Fantasy Romance Writing

Character Development & Plotting

L. A. Betford

The Betford Collection

Contents

Dear Writer,

The journey starts here with Fantasy Romance Writing; Character Development and Plotting, a definitive guide designed to help you weave compelling romantic narratives through character development and meticulous plotting. This book is intended for authors, scriptwriters, game designers, and creatives of all stripes who wish to elevate their stories through well-realized characters and tightly woven romantic plots.

From creating engaging backstories to navigating character growth within a love story, these chapters will guide you to build characters that readers can root for. From the first meeting to the climactic resolution, learn how to construct a romantic plot that resonates and captivates, with each chapter devoted to different stages of the romantic journey.

Whether you're drafting your first love story or adding another title to your romance portfolio, feel free to jump between sections, cherry-pick the topics you need help with, or follow the book sequentially. Fantasy Romance Writing: Character Development and Plotting is here to aid and inspire your creative process, without imposing rigid rules or formulae.

To crafting love stories that linger in hearts!

Crafting Compelling Characters

Character Ideas

A brave warrior, skilled in combat and loyal to his kingdom.

A mysterious sorceress with a troubled past and powerful magical abilities.

A kind-hearted healer who seeks to help those in need.

A proud elven prince, fiercely protective of his people and traditions.

A cunning thief with a roguish charm and a soft spot for the protagonist.

A noble knight with a tragic past, seeking redemption and a new purpose in life.

A fierce dragon, feared and respected by all who dwell in the realm.

A wise old wizard, with knowledge and insights that may hold the key to defeating the antagonist.

A mischievous fairy, with a penchant for pranks and a knack for getting into trouble.

A powerful demon, with a tempting offer that may prove too difficult to resist.

A vengeful ghost, seeking justice for a past wrong.

A tragic vampire, cursed to wander the earth alone for eternity.

A loyal companion, whether animal or humanoid, who aids the protagonist on their journey.

A cunning political advisor, with ambitions of their own that may not align with the protagonist's goals.

A rival from the protagonist's past, who may serve as a foil or a challenge to overcome.

A mermaid, with a hauntingly beautiful voice and a dangerous allure.

A cursed prince, seeking a way to break the spell that has trapped him in his current form.

A misanthropic hermit, who lives alone in the forest and distrusts all outsiders.

A wise-cracking bard, whose songs and stories may hold more truth than anyone realizes.

An enchanted object, with a personality and a will of its own, that may prove to be the key to defeating the antagonist or achieving the protagonist's goals.

A shape-shifting druid, with a deep connection to nature and the elements.

A cursed princess, whose fate is tied to that of the protagonist's.

A powerful witch, feared and misunderstood by those around her.

A noble centaur, with a strong sense of justice and honor.

A mischievous imp, with a knack for causing trouble and stirring up drama.

A tragic angel, who has fallen from grace and seeks redemption.

A cunning goblin, with a talent for thievery and mischief.

A lonely werewolf, searching for a pack and a sense of belonging.

A charismatic pirate, with a heart of gold and a love for adventure.

A cursed knight, doomed to roam the land until he finds true love.

A powerful genie, with the ability to grant wishes but a hidden agenda of her own.

A wise oracle, with knowledge of the future and the power to change it.

A fierce minotaur, with a gruff exterior but a soft spot for the protagonist.

A charming court jester, with a quick wit and a hidden intelligence.

A proud sphinx, with a riddle that the protagonist must solve in order to gain her favor.

A haunted specter, who may hold the key to solving a mystery or achieving a goal.

A reclusive alchemist, who may hold the secret to unlocking great power or knowledge.

A noble samurai, with a strict code of honor and a deep respect for tradition.

A mischievous leprechaun, with a pot of gold and a love for pranks and trickery.

A gentle giant, feared by many but with a heart of gold.

A haunted doll, possessed by the spirit of a lost love.

A cursed merman, searching for a way to break the spell and return to his true form.

A cunning sphinx, with a riddle that the protagonist must solve to gain access to a valuable resource.

A lonely ghost, bound to a specific location and seeking release.

A wise dragon, who serves as a mentor and guide to the protagonist.

A fierce warrior princess, who must balance her duty to her people with her growing love for the protagonist.

A mischievous gremlin, with a talent for causing chaos and destruction.

A proud unicorn, with a magical horn that may hold the key to solving a mystery or defeating an enemy.

A mysterious selkie, with the ability to transform from a seal to a human and back again.

A powerful djinn, with the ability to grant wishes but a hidden price to pay.
A tragic banshee, whose wail foretells the death of those who hear it.

A cunning satyr, with a love of revelry and a hidden agenda.

A wise sage, with knowledge and insights that may help the protagonist in their quest.

A fierce harpy, feared by many but with a heart that may be won over by the protagonist.

A cursed faerie, searching for a way to break the spell and reclaim their true form.

A gentle nymph, with a love for nature and a deep connection to the earth.

A proud griffin, with the body of a lion and the wings of an eagle.

A mischievous pixie, with a love for practical jokes and a knack for getting into trouble.

A powerful witch queen, with the ability to control the elements and a thirst for power.

The Protagonist

Someone who is searching for love and connection in a world that is full of danger and uncertainty. Their journey may involve battles with dark forces, exploration of mystical lands, and the discovery of hidden powers, all while navigating the ups and downs of falling in love.

These are the main characters, often with unique talents or abilities, who drive the story forward. In a fantasy romance, there should be at least two protagonists, each playing a role in both the fantasy and romance aspects of the story.

Relatable Flaws and Vulnerabilities

Giving your protagonist flaws and vulnerabilities makes them more human and relatable. These imperfections can create interesting character arcs as they grow and overcome their challenges.

Insecurity

The protagonist may doubt their own abilities or worthiness, making them hesitant to pursue their goals or the love interest. This insecurity can stem from past experiences, societal expectations, or personal fears.

A mage who doubts their magical abilities due to a tragic incident in their past, causing them to be cautious in using their powers.

Fear of Abandonment or Rejection

The protagonist may have a deep-rooted fear of being abandoned or rejected, which can influence their relationships and decision-making.

A warrior who lost their family in a war is afraid of forming close relationships, fearing that they might lose their loved ones again.

Impulsiveness

The protagonist may be prone to making hasty decisions, which can lead to unintended consequences or conflicts with other characters.

A thief who acts on impulse, stealing a powerful artifact without considering the consequences, putting them and their love interest in danger.

Overprotectiveness

The protagonist may be overly protective of those they care about, leading to conflict or stifling the growth of their loved ones.

A skilled healer who is overly protective of their love interest, hindering the love interest's ability to face challenges and grow as a person.

<u>Emotional Guardedness</u>
The protagonist may have difficulty expressing their emotions or allowing themselves to be vulnerable, creating barriers in their romantic relationship.

A sorceress who keeps her emotions under control due to the volatility of her magic, struggling to open up to her love interest.

<u>Perfectionism</u>
The protagonist may have unrealistic expectations for themselves or others, causing them to be overly critical or self-sabotaging.

A nobleman who strives for perfection in everything he does, finding it difficult to accept his own shortcomings and those of his love interest.

<u>Jealousy or Possessiveness</u>
The protagonist may struggle with feelings of jealousy or possessiveness, leading to tension in their romantic relationship or conflicts with other characters.

A shapeshifter who becomes jealous when their love interest forms a close bond with another character, leading to misunderstandings and strain in their relationship.

Unique Abilities or Talents

In a fantasy setting, the protagonist might have magical powers, exceptional skills, or other unique abilities that set them apart. This can be a source of both pride and struggle, as they learn to harness and control their powers or talents.

<u>Elemental Control</u>
The protagonist can manipulate one or more natural elements, such as water, fire, earth, or air.

A protagonist who can control fire, using their powers to protect their people or keep their love interest safe.

Telepathy or Empathy
The protagonist can read the thoughts or emotions of others, which
can be both a blessing and a curse in their romantic relationships.
An empath who can sense the emotions of those around them,
struggling to maintain boundaries and avoid being overwhelmed by
the feelings of others.

Shapeshifting
The protagonist can transform into different forms, such as animals,
mythical creatures, or other people.

A protagonist who can transform into a dragon, grappling with the
duality of their human and dragon nature in their quest for love.

Healing Abilities
The protagonist can heal themselves or others, either through
magical or non-magical means.

A skilled healer who can mend wounds and cure illnesses, facing
the responsibility and burden of deciding who to save and who to
let go.

Enhanced Physical Abilities
The protagonist possesses exceptional strength, agility, or
endurance that sets them apart from others.

A warrior with extraordinary strength, using their power to protect
their love interest and their kingdom from threats.

Time Manipulation
The protagonist can manipulate time, such as slowing it down,
speeding it up, or traveling through it.

A time traveler who falls in love with someone from a different era,
facing the challenges of balancing their love and their responsibility
to the timeline.

Summoning or Conjuring
The protagonist can summon or conjure objects, creatures, or other
entities to aid them in their journey.

A sorcerer who can summon mythical creatures to fight by their side, struggling to control the power they wield.

Illusion or Invisibility
The protagonist can create illusions or become invisible, using these abilities for various purposes throughout their adventure.

A protagonist who can create illusions, using their power to deceive enemies or hide their true feelings from their love interest.

Strong Motivations and Goals
A compelling protagonist should have clear motivations and goals that drive their actions throughout the story.

Finding True Love
The protagonist may be on a quest to find their soulmate, driven by their belief in true love or a prophecy that foretells their romantic destiny.

A lonely prince, searching for the princess whose love will break an ancient curse and bring peace to his kingdom.

Protecting Loved Ones
The protagonist's primary motivation may be to protect their friends, family, or love interest from harm, often requiring them to make personal sacrifices or face their fears.

A warrior who must protect her love interest from a powerful enemy, even if it means putting her own life in danger.

Discovering Their True Identity
The protagonist could be on a journey to uncover their true heritage or purpose, driven by a desire to understand themselves and their place in the world.

An orphan with mysterious magical powers, determined to discover the truth about her origins and her connection to a lost magical kingdom.

Achieving Personal Growth
The protagonist may be striving to overcome personal challenges, such as mastering their magical abilities, conquering their fears, or learning to trust others.

A mage who must learn to control his volatile magic to protect those he cares about, facing his own insecurities and self-doubt in the process.

Restoring Balance or Peace
The protagonist might be driven to restore balance or peace to their world, whether by defeating an evil force, uniting warring factions, or solving a magical crisis.

A diplomat tasked with brokering peace between two feuding magical races, finding love and understanding in the process.

Seeking Redemption or Forgiveness
The protagonist may be on a quest for redemption or forgiveness, either for their own past actions or for those of someone close to them.

A former assassin seeking to atone for her past deeds, determined to use her skills to save lives rather than take them.

Achieving a Personal Ambition
The protagonist might have a specific ambition, such as becoming a renowned knight, uncovering ancient knowledge, or achieving mastery in their magical discipline.

An aspiring sorceress who dreams of becoming a member of an elite magical council, facing both romantic and magical challenges on her path to success.

Depth and Complexity
A well-rounded protagonist should have a rich inner life, with thoughts, emotions, and beliefs that inform their actions. By giving your protagonist a strong sense of self, they will feel more real and engaging to the reader.

Define Their Core Values and Beliefs
Determine the values and beliefs that are most important to your protagonist. These can be shaped by their upbringing, culture, or personal experiences and can influence their decisions and actions throughout the story.

A protagonist who values loyalty and honesty, struggling to reconcile these values with their love interest's secretive past.

Explore Their Fears and Desires
Understand your protagonist's deepest fears and desires, as these can drive their actions and create emotional stakes in the story.

A protagonist who fears losing control of their magic, driven to find a way to master their powers and protect those they love.

Develop Their Interests and Passions
Give your protagonist interests and passions outside of their romantic relationship, making them feel more like a real person.

A protagonist who is an avid reader and collector of rare books, using their knowledge to solve mysteries and navigate the challenges they face.

Show Their Emotional Reactions
Allow your protagonist to experience a range of emotions, from joy and love to anger and sadness. Show their emotional reactions to different situations, revealing their vulnerabilities and strengths.

A protagonist who struggles to control their anger, learning to channel their emotions into constructive action as the story progresses.

Create Internal Conflicts
Develop internal conflicts within your protagonist that create tension and complexity, as they struggle to reconcile opposing desires, beliefs, or emotions.

A protagonist torn between their duty to their kingdom and their love for a person from a rival nation, grappling with their conflicting loyalties.

<u>Establish Their Backstory</u>
Develop your protagonist's backstory, including their family, upbringing, and formative experiences, to provide context for their actions and emotions.

A protagonist who was abandoned as a child and raised by a group of magical outcasts, shaping their sense of self and their views on love and acceptance.

<u>Use Introspection and Self-Reflection</u>
Show your protagonist engaging in introspection and self-reflection, as they examine their thoughts, feelings, and motivations throughout the story.

A protagonist who contemplates the nature of love and sacrifice, questioning whether they can truly give up their own happiness for the greater good.

Adaptability and Growth
An intriguing protagonist should be capable of change, growth, and development throughout the story.

<u>Overcoming Personal Flaws</u>
The protagonist may struggle with a personal flaw that impacts their relationships, their abilities, or their self-image. As they confront this flaw, they can grow and change for the better.

A protagonist with trust issues learns to open up and rely on others, ultimately strengthening their relationships and allowing them to succeed in their goals.

<u>Learning From Mistakes</u>
The protagonist may make mistakes that have consequences for themselves or others. Through reflection and learning, they can change their behavior and make better choices in the future.

A protagonist who acts impulsively, causing harm to their love interest, learns the importance of patience and forethought, ultimately becoming more responsible and thoughtful.

Adapting to New Challenges
The protagonist may face new challenges or situations that force
them to adapt their skills, beliefs, or attitudes in order to overcome
obstacles and achieve their goals.

A non-magical protagonist thrown into a magical world learns to
navigate its rules and customs, ultimately discovering their own
latent magical abilities and using them to save their love interest.

Developing Emotional Resilience
The protagonist may face emotional hardships or trauma that test
their resilience and force them to confront their vulnerabilities,
ultimately emerging stronger and more self-aware.

A protagonist who suffers a devastating loss learns to cope with
grief and finds new sources of strength and support, deepening
their emotional resilience and capacity for love.

Confronting Moral Dilemmas
The protagonist may face moral dilemmas that challenge their
values and force them to reevaluate their beliefs, leading to
personal growth and change.

A protagonist who must choose between their duty to their
kingdom and their love for a person from a rival nation, ultimately
learning the importance of compromise and understanding.

Building Relationships
The protagonist may develop new relationships or deepen existing
ones, leading to personal growth as they learn to navigate the
complexities of love, friendship, and trust.

A protagonist who begins the story as a loner learns the value of
friendship and teamwork, ultimately finding love and forming
lasting connections with others.

Achieving Self-Acceptance
The protagonist may struggle with self-acceptance, coming to terms
with their flaws, abilities, or identity, ultimately embracing their
true self and finding happiness.

18

A protagonist who initially denies their magical heritage learns to accept and embrace their powers, ultimately using them to save their world and find love.

Chemistry with the Love Interest

In a fantasy romance novel, the relationship between the protagonist and the love interest is a central aspect of the story. To make this relationship compelling, the protagonist should have strong chemistry with the love interest, as well as emotional depth and a genuine connection that goes beyond physical attraction.

Shared Experiences

The protagonist and love interest bond over shared experiences, such as facing challenges or overcoming obstacles together, which strengthen their emotional connection.

A protagonist and love interest who must work together to solve a magical mystery, gradually growing closer as they face challenges and uncover secrets together.

Complementary Personalities

The protagonist and love interest have complementary personalities, with each character's strengths balancing the other's weaknesses, creating a dynamic and engaging relationship.

A shy, introverted protagonist who finds courage and confidence in their outgoing, charismatic love interest, while the love interest learns the value of introspection and empathy from the protagonist.

Intellectual Connection

The protagonist and love interest share an intellectual connection, bonding over their shared interests, passions, or expertise, which adds depth to their relationship.

A protagonist who is a scholar of ancient magic finds a love interest who shares their passion for uncovering lost knowledge, engaging in deep discussions, and collaborating on research.

Emotional Vulnerability

The protagonist and love interest demonstrate emotional vulnerability with one another, revealing their fears, insecurities, and innermost thoughts, which fosters a deeper emotional connection.

A protagonist with a tragic past finds solace and understanding in their love interest, who has also experienced loss, leading to a bond based on empathy and shared grief.

Respect and Admiration

The protagonist and love interest show respect and admiration for each other's abilities, accomplishments, or character traits, reinforcing their emotional connection and fostering mutual admiration.

A warrior protagonist who admires the resilience and intelligence of their love interest, a skilled strategist, while the love interest respects the protagonist's strength and determination.

Trust and Loyalty

The protagonist and love interest develop trust and loyalty towards one another, creating a strong foundation for their relationship and allowing them to face challenges together.

A protagonist who initially struggles to trust their love interest due to past betrayals, gradually learning to rely on them as they prove their loyalty and commitment.

Conflict and Resolution

The protagonist and love interest experience conflicts, misunderstandings, or disagreements that test their relationship, ultimately resolving their issues and growing stronger as a result.

A protagonist and love interest who have opposing views on a political issue, engaging in passionate debates, and ultimately finding common ground or learning to respect their differences.

Moral Compass

A protagonist with a strong sense of right and wrong, or one who struggles with moral dilemmas, can make for a more engaging and complex character. This can add tension to both the romantic and fantasy aspects of the story.

Clear Moral Code

The protagonist has a clear moral code rooted in their upbringing, culture, or personal beliefs, which guides their decisions and actions throughout the story.

A protagonist who was raised to uphold the values of honor, loyalty, and justice, struggling to maintain these ideals in a world filled with corruption and deceit.

Challenging Circumstances

The protagonist faces circumstances that challenge their sense of right and wrong, forcing them to question their beliefs or make difficult choices.

A protagonist who discovers their kingdom is built on the suffering of others, grappling with whether to expose the truth or maintain the status quo for the sake of stability.

Conflicting Loyalties

The protagonist experiences conflicting loyalties, torn between their love interest and their duty to their family, friends, or kingdom, which creates moral dilemmas and tests their character.

A protagonist who falls in love with an enemy spy, struggling to reconcile their love with their duty to protect their people.

Temptation and Corruption

The protagonist faces temptation or corruption, battling against their darker impulses or external forces that seek to manipulate or control them.

A protagonist who gains immense power and must choose between using it for personal gain or upholding their moral principles.

Sacrifice and Loss
The protagonist must make sacrifices or suffer losses in order to stay true to their sense of right and wrong, which adds emotional depth and complexity to their character.

A protagonist who sacrifices their own happiness to protect their love interest or to save their kingdom from destruction.

Moral Growth and Change
The protagonist undergoes moral growth and change throughout the story, learning from their mistakes or experiences and evolving their sense of right and wrong.

A protagonist who starts out as a selfish or ruthless character, gradually learning the importance of empathy, compassion, and selflessness through their relationships and experiences.

Ethical Dilemmas
The protagonist faces ethical dilemmas that force them to weigh the consequences of their actions and make difficult decisions, revealing the complexity of their character.

A protagonist who must decide whether to kill a villain to save their love interest, struggling with the morality of taking a life even to protect someone they love.

The Love Interest

Someone who provides a sense of connection and belonging for the protagonist in a world that can be unpredictable and frightening. They are often the driving force behind the protagonist's journey, providing motivation and support as they navigate the challenges of the fantasy world and their own emotions.

The characters who become romantically involved with the protagonists. They should be well-developed, with their own strengths and flaws, and should play an active role in the story.

Develop a Unique Personality

Just like your protagonist, your love interest should have a unique personality, complete with strengths, weaknesses, and quirks. This will make them more memorable and appealing to readers.

Unusual Profession or Skills
Give the love interest a unique profession or set of skills that make them stand out and contribute to the story.

A love interest who is a talented alchemist, using their knowledge to create magical elixirs that assist the protagonist on their quest.

Distinctive Appearance
Create a memorable physical appearance for the love interest that highlights their personality or magical abilities.

A love interest with striking, mismatched eyes that signify their dual magical heritage, sparking curiosity and intrigue.

Quirky Personality Traits
Incorporate quirky personality traits or habits that make the love interest memorable and endearing to the protagonist and the reader.

A love interest who is charmingly clumsy, often causing minor accidents but always managing to recover with grace and humor.

Contrasting Demeanor
Create a love interest with a demeanor that contrasts the protagonist's, adding depth to their relationship and highlighting their individual personalities.

A reserved, analytical love interest who complements the protagonist's impulsive and passionate nature, providing balance and stability.

Hidden Talents or Interests
Give the love interest hidden talents or interests that surprise the protagonist and the reader, revealing unexpected layers to their character.

A love interest who is secretly a skilled musician, using their talent to express their emotions and connect with the protagonist on a deeper level.

Personal Values or Beliefs
Develop strong personal values or beliefs for the love interest that shape their decisions and actions throughout the story, creating a sense of depth and complexity.

A love interest who is fiercely loyal and protective, driven by their personal code of honor and duty to defend their friends and loved ones.

Emotional Vulnerability
Show the love interest's emotional vulnerability, making them more relatable and allowing the protagonist and reader to connect with them on a deeper level.

A love interest who struggles with self-doubt and insecurity, gradually opening up to the protagonist and learning to trust in their own worth.

Give Them a Compelling Backstory
A well-developed love interest should have a rich backstory that informs their behavior and motivations.

Tragic Past
Give the love interest a tragic past that influences their current actions, beliefs, and emotional state, creating depth and empathy.

A love interest who lost their family in a magical disaster, leaving them with a deep mistrust of magic and a determination to prevent similar tragedies.

Unique Upbringing
Develop a unique upbringing for the love interest that sets them apart and influences their worldview and values.

A love interest raised by a society of secretive mages, instilling in them a strong sense of loyalty to their community but also a curiosity about the outside world.

Family Dynamics
Create complex family dynamics that shape the love interest's personality and relationships, adding emotional depth to their character.

A love interest with a strained relationship with their overbearing, aristocratic parents, who disapprove of their unconventional passions and ambitions.

Personal Achievements or Failures
Include significant personal achievements or failures in the love interest's past that have shaped their self-image and motivations.

A love interest who was once a celebrated warrior but failed to protect a loved one, leading them to renounce their former life and seek redemption.

Romantic History
Develop the love interest's romantic history, which can create opportunities for conflict, growth, or understanding within the protagonist's relationship.

A love interest with a past relationship that ended painfully, making them hesitant to open their heart to the protagonist but ultimately deepening their connection as they learn to trust again.

Secrets Or Hidden Past
Give the love interest a secret or hidden past that gradually comes to light, creating intrigue and tension within the story.

A love interest who is revealed to be a fugitive from a powerful magical organization, forcing them to confront their past and protect those they care about.

<u>Connection to the Fantasy World</u>
Incorporate elements from the fantasy world into the love interest's backstory, highlighting their role within the larger setting and magical system.

A love interest who is the last descendant of an ancient line of dragon riders, tasked with protecting a sacred artifact and facing the responsibilities of their heritage.

Establish Their Goals and Motivations

Your love interest should have their own goals and motivations outside of the romantic relationship, making them a fully realized character with a sense of agency.

<u>Personal Ambition</u>
The love interest has a personal ambition or dream they are working towards, which drives their actions and decisions.

A love interest who aspires to become a renowned bard, traveling the world to collect stories and perform in prestigious venues.

<u>Family Obligations</u>
The love interest has family obligations or responsibilities that influence their choices and priorities.

A love interest who is the heir to a noble house, struggling to balance their duty to their family with their own desires and the romantic relationship.

<u>Quest for Knowledge</u>
The love interest is on a quest for knowledge or understanding, which shapes their actions and interests throughout the story.

A love interest who is a scholar of ancient magic, driven by a desire to uncover lost secrets and decipher mysterious artifacts.

<u>Moral or Ethical Cause</u>
The love interest is motivated by a moral or ethical cause, championing a particular issue or seeking to right a perceived wrong.

A love interest who fights for social justice and equality, working to dismantle oppressive systems and create a better world for all.

Redemption or atonement
The love interest seeks redemption or atonement for past mistakes or failures, driving them to make amends or prove themselves.

A love interest who was once a notorious thief, now seeking to repay their debts to society by helping those in need and protecting the innocent.

Loyalty to Friends or Allies
The love interest is motivated by loyalty to their friends or allies, willing to go to great lengths to support and protect them.

A love interest who is a member of a close-knit band of adventurers, driven by their commitment to their companions and their shared cause.

Pursuit of Power or Influence
The love interest seeks power or influence, whether for personal gain, to protect others, or to enact change.

A love interest who desires to rise through the ranks of a powerful magical organization, hoping to reform it from within and put an end to its corrupt practices.

Create Chemistry with the Protagonist
The love interest should have strong chemistry with the protagonist, sharing interests, values, or experiences that bring them together and make their relationship believable and engaging.

Shared Interests or Passions
The protagonist and love interest bond over shared interests or passions, which bring them closer and provide common ground for their relationship.

Both characters are skilled musicians, finding solace and connection through their love for music and often performing together.

Complementary Personalities
The protagonist and love interest have complementary
personalities that balance each other out, creating a dynamic that
feels natural and engaging.

The protagonist is impulsive and passionate, while the love interest
is calm and analytical, helping them to navigate challenges together
and learn from one another.

Emotional Vulnerability
The protagonist and love interest open up to each other about their
fears, insecurities, or past traumas, deepening their emotional
connection and building trust.

Both characters have experienced loss and find solace in confiding
in each other, gradually healing and growing stronger together.

Shared Experiences or Challenges
The protagonist and love interest face shared experiences or
challenges that bring them closer together and test their bond.

Both characters embark on a dangerous quest, relying on each
other's strengths and abilities to overcome obstacles and grow as a
team.

Banter and Playfulness
The protagonist and love interest engage in playful banter or
teasing, showcasing their rapport and mutual affection.

The characters often engage in witty verbal sparring, challenging
each other's intellect and sparking a flirtatious dynamic.

Shared Values or Beliefs
The protagonist and love interest bond over shared values or
beliefs, which serve as the foundation for their relationship.

Both characters are deeply committed to justice and equality,
working together to fight against oppression and make the world a
better place.

<u>Sacrifice and Support</u>
The protagonist and love interest demonstrate their love and commitment by making sacrifices or providing support for each other, reinforcing their emotional bond.

The protagonist risks their life to save the love interest from danger, while the love interest provides emotional support and encouragement during the protagonist's darkest moments.

Make Them Flawed and Relatable

Like any well-rounded character, the love interest should have flaws and vulnerabilities that make them human and relatable. This can also create opportunities for conflict and growth within the relationship.

<u>Fear of Commitment</u>
The love interest struggles with commitment due to past relationship experiences, leading to hesitations and doubts that create tension in the relationship.

The love interest's past heartbreak makes them wary of opening up to the protagonist, causing misunderstandings and emotional distance that they must work through together.

<u>Insecurity or Self-Doubt</u>
The love interest grapples with insecurity or self-doubt, which can lead to conflicts or misunderstandings in the relationship.

The love interest struggles with feelings of inadequacy in comparison to the protagonist's magical abilities, causing them to push the protagonist away or act defensively.

<u>Stubbornness or Pride</u>
The love interest's stubbornness or pride creates friction in the relationship, as they may struggle to compromise or admit when they are wrong.

The love interest's pride prevents them from accepting help or admitting their feelings for the protagonist, leading to tension and obstacles that must be overcome.

Trust Issues
The love interest has trust issues, making it difficult for them to fully open up to the protagonist and creating opportunities for growth and emotional depth.

The love interest's secretive past causes them to be guarded and suspicious, requiring the protagonist to earn their trust and break down their emotional barriers.

Overprotectiveness
The love interest's overprotectiveness can create conflict and tension in the relationship, as they may struggle to balance their desire to protect the protagonist with respecting their autonomy.

The love interest's fierce protectiveness leads them to interfere with the protagonist's choices or decisions, sparking disagreements and forcing them to find a balance between love and respect.

Jealousy or Possessiveness
The love interest may struggle with jealousy or possessiveness, which can create conflicts and opportunities for growth within the relationship.

The love interest's jealousy over the protagonist's close friendship with another character leads to tension and mistrust, requiring both characters to address their insecurities and strengthen their emotional connection.

Impulsiveness or Recklessness
The love interest's impulsiveness or recklessness can create tension in the relationship, as their actions may have unintended consequences or put themselves or others in danger.

The love interest's impulsivity causes them to make a risky decision that puts them in harm's way, leading the protagonist to confront them about their behavior and work together to navigate the consequences.

Allow for Character Growth

The love interest should also be capable of change and growth throughout the story, whether that's overcoming personal obstacles, learning from mistakes, or evolving in response to new challenges.

Learning to Trust

The love interest overcomes trust issues by opening up to the protagonist and working through their fears and insecurities together.

The love interest gradually shares their painful past with the protagonist, learning to trust and rely on them as they face challenges together.

Confronting Personal Demons

The love interest faces their personal demons, such as past traumas, guilt, or fears, and learns to overcome them through self-reflection and support from the protagonist.

The love interest confronts their guilt over a past mistake and, with the protagonist's encouragement, seeks redemption by making amends and learning to forgive themselves.

Developing Emotional Intelligence

The love interest learns to better understand and express their emotions, leading to improved communication and a stronger emotional connection with the protagonist.

The love interest learns to recognize and express their feelings of jealousy, allowing them to address their insecurities and strengthen their bond with the protagonist.

Overcoming Stubbornness or Pride

The love interest learns to be more flexible and open-minded, accepting help and guidance from the protagonist and others.

The love interest overcomes their pride by admitting when they are wrong and learning to compromise, leading to a more balanced and supportive relationship with the protagonist.

Embracing Change or Personal Growth
The love interest faces new challenges or experiences that force them to adapt and grow as a person, ultimately becoming a stronger and more resilient individual.

The love interest is thrust into a leadership role, learning to overcome their self-doubt and take responsibility for their actions and decisions.

Strengthening Relationships
The love interest learns the value of friendship, trust, and loyalty, ultimately forming stronger bonds with the protagonist and other characters.

The love interest overcomes their initial wariness of the protagonist's friends, eventually forming meaningful connections and recognizing the importance of a support network.

Acknowledging and Overcoming Flaws
The love interest recognizes their flaws and takes steps to address and overcome them, demonstrating personal growth and emotional maturity.

The love interest acknowledges their overprotectiveness and learns to respect the protagonist's autonomy, ultimately fostering a healthier and more equal partnership.

Balance Their Role in the Story

While the love interest is an essential part of the romantic storyline, make sure they also contribute to other aspects of the plot. This will ensure they remain an integral part of the overall story and not solely defined by their relationship with the protagonist.

Independent Goals and Motivations
Ensure the love interest has their own goals and motivations outside of the romantic relationship, making them a fully realized character with a sense of agency.

The love interest is on a quest to restore their family's honor, giving them a personal storyline that intersects and intertwines with the protagonist's journey.

Involvement in the Plot
Integrate the love interest into the larger plot, allowing them to contribute to and influence the story's progression.

The love interest's knowledge of an ancient magical language proves vital to deciphering a mysterious prophecy that drives the main plot.

Dynamic Relationships with Other Characters
Create relationships between the love interest and other characters, adding depth and complexity to their characterization and interactions.

The love interest forms a close friendship with the protagonist's mentor, providing an additional layer of connection and emotional support within the story.

Overcoming Personal Obstacles
Include personal obstacles or challenges that the love interest must overcome, which parallel or complement the protagonist's own journey.

The love interest struggles with self-doubt and insecurity, learning to trust their abilities and instincts as they face challenges alongside the protagonist.

Shared Challenges or Quests
Involve the love interest and the protagonist in shared challenges or quests that test their bond and force them to work together as a team.

The love interest and protagonist must navigate a treacherous labyrinth to retrieve a powerful artifact, relying on their combined skills and strengths to overcome obstacles.

<u>Personal Growth and Development</u>
Allow the love interest to experience personal growth and development throughout the story, enhancing their character arc and making them a more dynamic and engaging presence.

The love interest learns to embrace their magical heritage and accept their true identity, ultimately becoming a more confident and self-assured individual.

<u>Opportunities For Heroism or Sacrifice</u>
Give the love interest opportunities to demonstrate their courage, commitment, or selflessness, showcasing their qualities beyond the romantic relationship.

The love interest sacrifices their own safety to protect the protagonist during a climactic battle, highlighting their bravery and devotion.

The Sidekick

A character who helps the protagonist grow and develop, both as a person and as a member of the fantasy world. They provide a sense of stability and support, even in the face of the most daunting challenges. This character assists, advises, or trains the protagonists in their journey. They are often wise and experienced in the ways of the world, providing valuable insights and guidance.

They act as a reliable mentor figure, offering their knowledge and expertise to help the hero navigate the complexities of the fantasy realm and overcome obstacles along the way. Their presence is instrumental in the protagonist's growth and serves as a source of strength and encouragement throughout their romantic quest.

Develop a Unique Personality

Give the sidekick a distinct personality that complements and contrasts with the protagonist and love interest. This will create interesting dynamics between the characters and allow the sidekick to bring out different aspects of the main characters' personalities.

Complementary Traits

Giving the sidekick traits that complement the protagonist or love interest can help to highlight their strengths and create a strong team dynamic.

If the protagonist is a brave warrior with little patience for strategy, the sidekick could be a skilled tactician, helping to plan their battles and mitigate the protagonist's impulsive nature.

Contrasting Traits

On the other hand, the sidekick can also have traits that contrast with the protagonist or love interest, which can create conflict and tension, but also growth opportunities for all characters.

If the protagonist is a stoic and serious character, the sidekick could be more light-hearted and jovial, which can lead to disagreements but also help the protagonist to lighten up and enjoy life more.

Different Background

The sidekick could come from a different social or cultural background than the protagonist and love interest, offering different perspectives and creating opportunities for them to learn from each other.

If the protagonist is a prince, the sidekick could be a commoner, providing a different view on the kingdom and its people, and helping the prince to understand and connect with his subjects.

Different Skills or Abilities

The sidekick could possess skills or abilities that the protagonist and love interest lack, making them indispensable.

If the protagonist is a skilled swordsman but lacks knowledge of magic, the sidekick could be a mage, providing magical assistance in their adventures.

<u>Different Moral Compass</u>
The sidekick could have a different moral or ethical compass, challenging the protagonist and love interest's beliefs and decisions.

If the protagonist is willing to do whatever it takes to achieve their goals, the sidekick could be more principled, questioning the protagonist's actions and pushing them to consider the moral implications of their choices.

Define Their Role

Determine the sidekick's role in the story. They could be a loyal friend, a source of comic relief, a mentor, a protector, or a combination of these roles. The sidekick's role will help define their actions and interactions throughout the story.

<u>Loyal Friend</u>
The sidekick can serve as a loyal friend to the protagonist, offering emotional support, encouragement, and companionship throughout their journey. Their loyalty could be demonstrated through their willingness to stick with the protagonist through thick and thin, and their actions would be guided by their concern for the protagonist's well-being.

If the protagonist is heartbroken over a conflict with the love interest, the sidekick might comfort them, offer advice, or help them find a way to resolve the conflict.

<u>Source of Comic Relief</u>
The sidekick can be a source of comic relief, lightening the mood during tense or dramatic moments with their humor or quirky behavior. This would be reflected in their dialogue, actions, and interactions with other characters.

In a high-stakes battle, the sidekick might accidentally trip over their own feet, or make a witty comment that brings a moment of levity to the situation.

<u>Mentor</u>
The sidekick can also serve as a mentor to the protagonist, offering wisdom and guidance based on their own experiences or knowledge. This would influence their interactions with the

protagonist, as they would often provide advice or insight, and it might also determine their role in the plot, as they could help the protagonist learn and grow.

If the protagonist struggles to control their magical abilities, the sidekick might teach them techniques to manage their powers.

Protector

The sidekick could act as a protector, using their skills or abilities to defend the protagonist from harm. This would define their actions in conflicts or dangerous situations, where they would often take on a defensive role.

If the protagonist is attacked by an enemy, the sidekick might step in to fight them off.

Combination of Roles

The sidekick could fulfill a combination of these roles, making them a multi-faceted character with a significant impact on the story. Their actions and interactions would be influenced by the different aspects of their role.

A sidekick who is both a loyal friend and a protector might not only support the protagonist emotionally but also defend them in battles.

Create a Strong Relationship

Establish a strong bond between the sidekick and the main characters. This relationship should be characterized by trust, respect, and mutual support. Shared experiences, common goals, or a shared past can help develop this bond.

Trust

Trust is a cornerstone of any close relationship, and it's particularly important in the dynamic between a sidekick and the main characters. This could be shown in how the main characters confide in the sidekick, rely on them in challenging situations, or entrust them with important tasks or secrets.

If the protagonist has a secret about their past or their powers, they might share it with the sidekick, demonstrating their trust in the sidekick's loyalty and discretion.

Respect
The main characters should also respect the sidekick, valuing their opinions, acknowledging their skills, and treating them as an equal partner. This could be reflected in how the main characters listen to the sidekick's advice, praise their accomplishments, or defend them against criticism.

If others dismiss the sidekick as incompetent or insignificant, the protagonist might stand up for them, showing their respect for the sidekick's abilities and character.

Mutual Support
The sidekick and the main characters should support each other, providing help, comfort, or encouragement when needed. This might be shown in how they comfort each other during difficult times, help each other overcome challenges, or celebrate each other's victories.

If the protagonist is facing a tough battle, the sidekick might offer to fight alongside them, or if the protagonist achieves a significant victory, the sidekick might be the first to congratulate them.

Shared Experiences
Shared experiences can strengthen the bond between the sidekick and the main characters, as they go through adventures, face dangers, or overcome obstacles together. These experiences can create shared memories, mutual understanding, and a sense of camaraderie.

If the sidekick and the protagonist embark on a dangerous quest together, the trials they face and the triumphs they achieve could bring them closer and deepen their bond.

Common Goals
Having common goals can also enhance the relationship between the sidekick and the main characters, as they work together

towards a shared objective. This can create opportunities for cooperation, teamwork, and mutual growth.

If the sidekick and the protagonist both aim to defeat the antagonist, their efforts to achieve this goal could foster collaboration and solidarity.

Shared Past
A shared past can provide a strong foundation for the relationship between the sidekick and the main characters. This could involve a shared history, common origins, or past experiences that have shaped them.

If the sidekick and the protagonist grew up in the same village or were both victims of the same tragedy, this shared past could create a strong bond between them.

Give Them Skills and Talents

Equip the sidekick with their own set of skills or talents that contribute to the story or aid the main characters in some way. These skills could be practical, like combat or healing, or more abstract, like wisdom or diplomacy.

Practical Skills
Giving the sidekick practical skills can make them a valuable asset to the main characters and the story. These skills can range from combat and healing to thievery and magical abilities.

A sidekick might be an expert swordsman, providing protection and tactical advice during battles. Or they might be a skilled healer, using their knowledge of herbs and magic to treat injuries and illnesses.

Abstract Skills
Abstract skills can also be useful, offering the main characters guidance, insight, or diplomatic solutions.

The sidekick might be a wise old sage, providing wisdom and advice to the protagonist during their journey. Or they might be a skilled diplomat, helping to negotiate treaties or navigate political intrigues.

Unique Talents

The sidekick could also have unique talents that set them apart and add an element of surprise or novelty to the story.

A sidekick might have the ability to communicate with animals, aiding the protagonist in gathering information or summoning help. Or they might be able to see the future, providing warnings or guidance to the main characters.

Role-Specific Skills

The sidekick's skills could be related to their role in the story or their background.

If the sidekick is a former thief, they might have stealth skills and a knack for disabling traps. If they're a scholar or a librarian, they could have vast knowledge of history, magic, or other relevant subjects.

Development of Skills

It's also important to show the sidekick developing their skills over the course of the story. This can provide a subplot of personal growth and a sense of progress.

The sidekick might start off as a novice magician, gradually learning to control their powers and becoming a competent spellcaster by the end of the story.

Establish Clear Motivations

The sidekick should have their own motivations, separate from those of the main characters.

Personal Goals

The sidekick might have personal goals that motivate them to join or stay with the protagonist. For instance, they might hope to prove their worth, seek redemption for past mistakes, or find a lost family member.

A sidekick could be motivated to join the protagonist in their quest because they believe it will lead them to a long-lost sibling they've been searching for.

<u>Sense of Duty</u>
The sidekick's motivations could stem from a sense of duty or obligation. This could be a duty to their homeland, their family, or the protagonist themselves.

A knight might serve as a sidekick to a royal protagonist out of a sworn duty to protect them. Or a sidekick could be motivated by a promise made to a loved one, to protect and guide the protagonist.

<u>Desire to Do What's Right</u>
The sidekick might be motivated by a strong moral compass or a desire to do what's right. They could be driven by a desire to see justice served, to protect innocent people, or to prevent a catastrophe.

A sidekick could join the protagonist in their fight against an evil empire because they believe it's the right thing to do, even if it puts them in danger.

<u>Personal Growth</u>
The sidekick's motivations could also be tied to their personal growth. They might wish to overcome their fears, grow stronger, or learn new skills.

A timid sidekick might be motivated to face their fears and prove their bravery by joining the protagonist's quest.

<u>Revenge or Vengeance</u>
A sidekick could be driven by a desire for revenge or vengeance. Perhaps the antagonist wronged them in the past, and they join the protagonist to settle the score.

If the antagonist destroyed the sidekick's home village, the sidekick might be motivated by a need for vengeance.

Provide a Backstory

Give the sidekick a well-developed backstory that explains who they are, where they come from, and how they became connected to the main characters. This backstory can offer opportunities for character development and plot progression.

Who They Are

The sidekick's backstory should explain their personality traits, attitudes, and values. This could involve significant events or experiences that shaped them.

A sidekick who is fiercely loyal to the protagonist might have been betrayed in the past, making them value loyalty even more.

Where They Come From

The sidekick's origins can tell a lot about their character. They could come from a different social class, culture, or region than the protagonist, which could explain their unique perspectives or skills.

A sidekick from a rural, farming community might have practical survival skills and a down-to-earth, pragmatic worldview that contrasts with a protagonist from a more privileged, urban background.

Connection to the Main Characters

The backstory should also explain how the sidekick became involved with the main characters. They might have a shared past, a mutual friend, or a common enemy.

The sidekick could be the protagonist's childhood friend who stood by them through thick and thin, or they might have joined the protagonist's cause after being saved by them.

Opportunities for Character Development

A well-crafted backstory can offer many opportunities for character development. It can provide a basis for the sidekick's motivations, fears, and desires, which can evolve over the course of the story.

A sidekick with a tragic past might initially be driven by revenge but gradually learn to let go of their anger and find peace.

Plot Progression

The sidekick's backstory can also contribute to the plot. Secrets from their past could lead to unexpected twists, or their connections to other characters could advance the storyline.

The sidekick might have insider knowledge about the antagonist's plans or weaknesses due to a past association, which could be crucial in the story's climax.

Include Growth and Development

Just like the main characters, the sidekick should grow and develop throughout the story. They might learn new skills, overcome personal challenges, or evolve in their beliefs or attitudes.

Learning New Skills

The sidekick can acquire new skills or improve existing ones as the story progresses. This could be a result of training, self-study, or learning from other characters.

The sidekick might start the story as a novice archer and become a master marksman by the end, or they might learn magical spells or abilities that they didn't possess at the beginning.

Overcoming Personal Challenges

The sidekick might face personal hurdles or struggles, which they gradually overcome. This could involve confronting fears, resolving internal conflicts, or overcoming personal flaws.

A sidekick who is initially afraid of magic could slowly learn to understand and embrace it, or a sidekick who struggles with self-doubt could grow more confident and assertive.

Evolving Beliefs or Attitudes

The sidekick's beliefs, attitudes, or worldview could change over time. This could be a result of new experiences, interactions with other characters, or introspection.

A sidekick who initially sees the world in black-and-white terms could learn to appreciate its complexities and nuances, or a sidekick who starts off as cynical or jaded could rediscover hope and optimism.

Ensure They Contribute to the Plot

The sidekick should play a significant role in the plot, whether it's helping the main characters overcome challenges, providing crucial information, or influencing the main characters' decisions or actions.

<u>Helping the Main Characters Overcome Challenges</u>
The sidekick could play a crucial role in helping the main characters overcome obstacles or defeat enemies. For instance, the sidekick might use their unique skills to disarm a trap, distract a villain, or heal an injured character.

In a crucial battle, it might be the sidekick's knowledge of a specific magic that turns the tide in their favor.

<u>Providing Crucial Information</u>
The sidekick could provide important information or insights that the main characters lack. This could involve sharing knowledge about the world, revealing hidden truths, or pointing out things the main characters have overlooked.

The sidekick might know the secret weakness of an enemy or the location of a hidden treasure.

<u>Influencing the Main Characters' Decisions or Actions</u>
The sidekick could influence the main characters in subtle or overt ways. They might offer advice, challenge the main characters' beliefs, or serve as a moral compass.

A sidekick might persuade the protagonist to take a risk for love, or they might encourage the love interest to trust the protagonist.

The Mentor

Someone who helps the protagonist grow and develop, both as a person and as a member of the fantasy world. They provide a sense of stability and support, even in the face of the most daunting challenges.

A character who assists, advises, or trains the protagonists in their journey. They are often wise and experienced in the ways of the world, providing valuable insights and guidance.

Wisdom and Experience

A mentor should have a wealth of knowledge and experience,
which they can impart to the protagonist or love interest, guiding
them on their journey and helping them make informed decisions.

Sharing Lore or History

The mentor could recount stories or legends that help the
protagonist or love interest understand the world they inhabit and
the challenges they face.

The mentor explains the history of a magical artifact, giving the
protagonist insight into its importance and the dangers they may
encounter while seeking it.

Teaching A Skill or Ability

The mentor may teach the protagonist or love interest a valuable
skill, ability, or magical power, helping them grow stronger and
more capable.

The mentor trains the protagonist in sword fighting, enabling them
to defend themselves and others during their journey.

Providing Advice or Guidance

The mentor can offer advice or guidance to the protagonist or love
interest during times of doubt, helping them make informed
decisions and navigate complex situations.

The mentor counsels the protagonist on how to approach
diplomatic negotiations with a rival kingdom, ensuring a peaceful
resolution.

Demonstrating Expertise

Show the mentor's knowledge and experience in action by having
them solve problems or overcome challenges using their unique
skills and abilities.

The mentor deciphers an ancient riddle, opening a hidden passage
that leads the protagonist and love interest to a crucial discovery.

Serving as a Role Model
The mentor's past experiences, successes, and failures can serve as a valuable example for the protagonist or love interest, inspiring them to learn from the mentor's wisdom.

The mentor shares their own experiences with love and loss, helping the protagonist navigate their feelings for the love interest and understand the importance of vulnerability and trust.

Offering Emotional Support
The mentor can provide emotional support and encouragement, helping the protagonist or love interest face their fears, embrace their feelings, and overcome personal challenges.

The mentor reassures the love interest when they doubt their own abilities, helping them gain confidence and embrace their potential.

Emotional Support

A mentor can provide emotional support, encouragement, and guidance to the characters, helping them navigate personal struggles, romantic entanglements, and the challenges they face throughout the story.

Comfort During Heartache
The mentor can offer a listening ear and wise advice when the protagonist or love interest is dealing with heartache or emotional pain.

The mentor comforts the protagonist after a painful argument with the love interest, helping them see the situation from a different perspective and encouraging open communication.

Encouragement During Self-Doubt
When the protagonist or love interest faces self-doubt, the mentor can provide reassurance and encouragement, bolstering their confidence.

The mentor reminds the love interest of their accomplishments and inner strength, helping them overcome their feelings of inadequacy and self-doubt.

Guidance Through Difficult Choices

The mentor can help the characters navigate difficult decisions by sharing their own experiences and offering guidance without imposing their own beliefs.

The mentor shares a personal story about a tough decision they faced in the past, helping the protagonist weigh the pros and cons of a choice that could impact their relationship and their future.

Support During Emotional Turmoil

The mentor can provide a safe space for the characters to express their emotions and fears, offering understanding and empathy.

The mentor listens as the protagonist vents their frustration and anger over a betrayal, validating their feelings and helping them process the situation.

Help in Resolving Conflicts

The mentor can assist the characters in resolving conflicts, guiding them towards effective communication, compromise, and understanding.

The mentor mediates a disagreement between the protagonist and love interest, encouraging them to express their feelings and listen to each other's perspectives.

Encouragement to Face Fears

The mentor can help the characters face their fears, providing support and encouragement as they confront difficult situations or personal demons.

The mentor encourages the love interest to confront their fear of abandonment, helping them build the courage to open up to the protagonist about their past.

Celebrating Successes

The mentor can be there to celebrate the characters' successes, reinforcing their achievements and helping them recognize their growth.

The mentor congratulates the protagonist for mastering a difficult magical technique, acknowledging their hard work and dedication.

A Unique Perspective

A good mentor can offer a unique perspective, often grounded in their own past experiences or cultural background, which can help the protagonist or love interest gain a broader understanding of the world and their place in it.

Cultural Insights
The mentor can share their cultural heritage and traditions, providing the protagonist or love interest with a deeper understanding of the diverse world they inhabit.

The mentor teaches the protagonist about the customs and beliefs of a neighboring kingdom, helping them better navigate cross-cultural interactions and alliances.

Lessons From History
The mentor can use their knowledge of history or past events to provide context for the protagonist or love interest's current challenges and decisions.

The mentor recounts the story of an ancient conflict that mirrors the protagonist's current situation, helping them understand the potential consequences of their actions and the importance of forging peaceful resolutions.

Philosophical Guidance
The mentor can offer philosophical insights or wisdom that challenge the protagonist or love interest's beliefs and assumptions, encouraging them to consider alternative viewpoints.

The mentor shares a parable about the nature of love and power, prompting the protagonist to reevaluate their priorities and consider the long-term impact of their choices.

Personal Experiences
The mentor can share their own personal experiences, including successes, failures, and life lessons, to guide the protagonist or love interest through similar challenges.

The mentor opens up about their own failed romance, offering valuable insights and advice to help the protagonist navigate their blossoming relationship with the love interest.

Unique Knowledge or Expertise

The mentor's specialized knowledge or expertise in a particular field can help the protagonist or love interest gain new perspectives on their own abilities or the challenges they face.

The mentor, an expert in magical creatures, teaches the love interest about the hidden world of magical fauna, expanding their understanding of the world's complexity and wonder.

Spiritual or Mystical Guidance

The mentor can provide spiritual or mystical guidance that helps the protagonist or love interest explore their own beliefs, values, and personal growth.

The mentor introduces the protagonist to an ancient meditation practice, helping them cultivate inner peace and self-awareness in the face of external challenges.

Flaws and Vulnerabilities

A well-rounded mentor should have their own flaws and vulnerabilities, making them a more relatable and human character.

These imperfections can also serve to highlight the mentor's growth and development throughout the story.

Past Mistakes

The mentor could have a history of poor decisions or mistakes that still haunt them. Their experiences can serve as valuable lessons for the protagonist and love interest, while also illustrating the mentor's own growth.

The mentor regrets a past decision that led to the loss of a loved one, and their journey to forgiveness and acceptance becomes a subplot within the story.

Emotional Vulnerability
The mentor may have difficulty expressing their emotions or opening up to others, making them appear distant or cold. As they learn to trust and confide in the protagonist or love interest, their emotional vulnerability becomes a source of growth.

The mentor struggles to express their pride and affection for the protagonist, but over time, they learn to be more open and emotionally available.

Personal Fears or Insecurities
The mentor might have their own fears or insecurities that they must confront and overcome throughout the story, allowing readers to witness their growth and transformation.

The mentor harbors a deep fear of failure, which they must confront and overcome to help the protagonist succeed in their quest.

Imperfect Judgment or Biases
The mentor may have their own biases or imperfect judgment that leads to misunderstandings or conflicts with the protagonist or love interest. These flaws can serve as opportunities for the mentor to learn and grow.

The mentor's distrust of a particular group or faction initially causes tension with the protagonist, but they eventually learn to challenge their preconceptions and develop a more open-minded perspective.

Overprotectiveness or Controlling Behavior
The mentor may be overly protective or controlling, struggling to allow the protagonist or love interest to make their own choices and learn from their mistakes. This flaw can be a source of conflict and growth for both the mentor and the characters they guide.

The mentor tries to shield the protagonist from a dangerous situation, but ultimately realizes that they must let the protagonist face challenges and grow independently.

<u>Physical Limitations or Weaknesses</u>
The mentor could have physical limitations or weaknesses that they must work around or overcome, demonstrating resilience and adaptability.

The mentor is blind but uses their other heightened senses to navigate the world and teach valuable lessons to the protagonist and love interest.

Conflict and Challenges

A mentor may not always agree with the protagonist or love interest, leading to conflict or challenges that test the characters' relationships and force them to confront their own beliefs or assumptions.

<u>Different Priorities</u>
The mentor and protagonist may have different priorities or values, leading to disagreements about the right course of action.

The mentor values tradition and order, while the protagonist is more focused on innovation and change, causing them to clash over how to handle a particular situation.

<u>Disapproval of Romantic Relationships</u>
The mentor may disapprove of the protagonist's romantic relationship with the love interest, believing it to be a distraction or hindrance to their quest.

The mentor discourages the protagonist from pursuing a relationship with the love interest, causing tension and forcing the protagonist to evaluate their feelings and priorities.

<u>Conflicting Strategies</u>
The mentor and protagonist may have opposing ideas on how to tackle a problem or challenge, leading to arguments and testing their trust in each other.

The mentor believes in diplomacy and negotiation, while the protagonist prefers a more direct and confrontational approach, resulting in a heated debate about how to resolve a conflict with an antagonist.

Differing Moral Beliefs
The mentor and the protagonist may have different moral beliefs, causing tension and forcing each character to examine their own values and motivations.

The mentor advocates for a utilitarian approach that may harm innocent people for the greater good, while the protagonist insists on protecting all lives, leading to a moral dilemma and a rift between them.

Challenging the Mentor's Authority
The protagonist or love interest may question the mentor's authority or wisdom, leading to conflicts that test their relationship and force them to reevaluate their roles.

The protagonist discovers that the mentor has been withholding crucial information, causing them to question the mentor's intentions and confront them about their secrecy.

Personal Disagreements
The mentor and the protagonist or love interest may have personal disagreements or clashes in personality, which can create tension and force them to work through their differences.

The mentor's strict and disciplined demeanor clashes with the love interest's free-spirited and rebellious nature, leading to arguments that force both characters to confront their assumptions about each other and find common ground.

A Sense of Mystery or Intrigue

A good mentor can have an air of mystery or intrigue, with hidden depths or a mysterious past that adds complexity to their character and piques the reader's curiosity.

Unrevealed Past Connections
The mentor may have a hidden connection to one of the other characters, which is only gradually revealed throughout the story.

The mentor is revealed to have once been close friends with the story's antagonist, raising questions about their past relationship and motivations.

Secret Identity
The mentor could have a secret identity, perhaps as a member of a clandestine organization or a figure of legend.

The mentor is secretly a member of a powerful and mysterious magical order, their true role within the group slowly coming to light as the story unfolds.

Mysterious Abilities
The mentor may possess mysterious abilities or powers that are not immediately apparent, intriguing the reader and the other characters.

The mentor occasionally displays knowledge or skills beyond what is expected of them, hinting at a hidden past as a powerful mage or warrior.

Ambiguous Intentions
The mentor's intentions or loyalties may be unclear or ambiguous, leaving the reader and other characters uncertain about their true motives.

The mentor seems to be helping the protagonist, but occasionally takes actions that could be interpreted as undermining their efforts, creating tension and uncertainty about their true intentions.

Lost Love or Tragedy
The mentor may have a tragic or mysterious past involving a lost love, which is slowly revealed throughout the story.

The mentor is haunted by the memory of a past lover, whose untimely death remains shrouded in mystery and impacts the mentor's decisions and actions.

Unexplained Absence or Disappearance
The mentor may have a history of unexplained absences or disappearances, adding an element of mystery to their character.

The mentor occasionally vanishes without explanation, only to reappear with new insights or knowledge that aid the protagonist, leaving the reader curious about their whereabouts during these absences.

<u>Rumors and Legends</u>
Other characters may share rumors or legends about the mentor, hinting at a mysterious past that is not fully explained or confirmed.

Whispers and stories circulate about the mentor's legendary exploits, creating an air of intrigue and leaving the reader eager to learn more about their true history.

Sacrifice or Loss

A mentor may be willing to make sacrifices or endure personal loss in service of the greater good or to protect the protagonist and love interest, highlighting their strength of character and commitment to their cause.

<u>Self-Sacrifice</u>
The mentor willingly puts their own life on the line to protect the protagonist or love interest from harm, demonstrating their selflessness and commitment to the characters.

The mentor steps in front of a deadly magical attack meant for the protagonist, showing their willingness to risk their life for the ones they care about.

<u>Sacrificing Personal Desires</u>
The mentor may choose to give up something they deeply desire in order to further the greater good or to help the protagonist and love interest.

The mentor relinquishes a chance at reuniting with a long-lost love in order to continue guiding the protagonist on their journey.

<u>Enduring Hardship</u>
The mentor may endure physical or emotional pain, loss, or hardship in order to protect the protagonist and love interest or support their cause.

The mentor allows themselves to be captured and tortured by the enemy to buy time for the protagonist and love interest to escape, demonstrating their resilience and commitment.

Letting Go of Personal Attachments
The mentor might have to sever personal ties or relationships to ensure the protagonist and love interest's success or safety.

The mentor decides to leave behind a close friend or family member in order to continue guiding the protagonist, emphasizing their dedication to the cause.

Forgoing Personal Power or Status
The mentor may choose to relinquish power or status to support the greater good or the protagonist's journey.

The mentor turns down a prestigious position within a magical council to remain by the protagonist's side as their guide and protector.

Risking Reputation or Standing
The mentor could risk their reputation or standing within their community to defend the protagonist and love interest or to uphold their beliefs.

The mentor publicly defends the protagonist's controversial actions, even though it may damage their own reputation among their peers.

Accepting Personal Loss
The mentor may accept personal loss, such as the destruction of their home or the death of a loved one, as a consequence of their commitment to the greater good and the protagonist's journey.

The mentor's home is destroyed during a battle, but they accept the loss and continue to guide the protagonist, demonstrating their unwavering dedication.

The Antagonist

Someone who creates tension and conflict, pushing the protagonist to grow and develop in unexpected ways. They are often the source of the most exciting and dramatic moments in the story, as the protagonist battles to overcome their influence and achieve their goals.

The character or force that opposes the protagonists, creating conflict and tension in the story. This can be a single individual or a group, and they may have a personal connection to the protagonists or their love interests.

Clear Motivations

Give the antagonist clear motivations and goals that drive their actions throughout the story. Their motivations could be rooted in ambition, revenge, a desire for power, or even a misguided belief that they are working for the greater good.

<u>Revenge</u>
The antagonist seeks revenge on the protagonist or love interest for a past wrong or perceived slight.

The antagonist blames the protagonist for the death of a loved one and is determined to make them suffer in return.

<u>Power</u>
The antagonist desires power, whether political, magical, or social, and will stop at nothing to achieve it.

The antagonist wants to overthrow the ruling monarchy and take the throne, bringing the protagonist and love interest into conflict as they try to prevent this.

<u>Jealousy</u>
The antagonist is driven by jealousy towards the protagonist or love interest, either for their abilities, relationships, or status.

The antagonist envies the protagonist's magical talents and seeks to undermine them at every turn.

<u>Love Rivalry</u>
The antagonist is in love with the protagonist or love interest and sees the other character as competition, creating romantic conflict.

The antagonist is in love with the love interest and tries to sabotage the developing relationship between the protagonist and the love interest.

<u>Misguided Belief</u>
The antagonist genuinely believes that their actions are for the greater good, even if their methods are questionable.

The antagonist wants to rid the world of magic, believing it to be the source of all suffering, and clashes with the magically-gifted protagonist.

Redemption
The antagonist seeks redemption for past mistakes or sins and will go to great lengths to right their wrongs, even if it brings them into conflict with the protagonist.

The antagonist wants to make amends for past misdeeds, but their efforts to atone inadvertently disrupt the protagonist's life or mission.

Personal Ambition
The antagonist is driven by personal ambition, which could be achieving a specific goal or proving themselves to others.

The antagonist wants to be recognized as the greatest warrior in the realm and challenges the protagonist in a high-stakes duel to prove their worth.

Backstory
Develop a compelling backstory for the antagonist that explains how they came to be the person they are. Their past experiences, relationships, and traumas can shape their motivations, desires, and worldview.

Tragic Past
The antagonist has experienced a significant loss or tragedy that has shaped their worldview and motivations.

The antagonist's village was destroyed by magic users, leading them to develop a deep hatred for magic and a desire to eradicate it from the world.

Betrayal
The antagonist has been betrayed by someone close to them, fueling their need for revenge or mistrust of others.

The antagonist was once close friends with the protagonist, but a betrayal caused their relationship to fracture, turning them into bitter enemies.

Unrequited Love
The antagonist has experienced unrequited love, which has driven them to desperate or destructive actions.

The antagonist has loved the protagonist from afar for years but, feeling rejected, they become consumed by jealousy and spite.

Abusive Upbringing
The antagonist grew up in an abusive or oppressive environment, shaping their beliefs and actions as an adult.

The antagonist was raised by a cruel and domineering parent, leading them to seek power and control over others as a means of feeling secure.

Quest for Power
The antagonist's pursuit of power or status has consumed them, driving them to take drastic and morally ambiguous actions.

The antagonist was once a loyal servant to the kingdom but hungry for power, they turned against their ruler and sought to claim the throne.

Failed Ambition
The antagonist experienced a failure or setback in their past that has left them bitter and resentful.

The antagonist was once a skilled mage but lost their powers in a magical accident, leading them to resent those who still possess magical abilities.

Unintended Consequences
The antagonist's actions in the past had unintended consequences that led to suffering or harm, causing them to seek redemption or retribution.

The antagonist accidentally caused the death of an innocent person while trying to protect their family, leading them on a dark path of revenge against those they hold responsible.

Strengths and Abilities

Make the antagonist formidable by providing them with unique skills, talents, or magical powers that challenge the protagonist and love interest. Their abilities should not only create external conflict but also force the protagonist and love interest to confront their own weaknesses and fears.

Master Strategist
The antagonist is an expert in devising intricate plans and manipulating others, forcing the protagonist and love interest to outwit them at every turn.

The antagonist orchestrates a complex web of political intrigue that threatens the protagonist's kingdom and their relationship with the love interest.

Skilled Combatant
The antagonist is a highly skilled warrior, making them a dangerous physical adversary for the protagonist and love interest.

The antagonist is an undefeated swordsman who challenges the protagonist to a duel with the love interest's life hanging in the balance.

Powerful Magic User
The antagonist possesses formidable magical abilities that the protagonist and love interest must learn to counter or defend against.

The antagonist can control the elements, summoning storms, or earthquakes to wreak havoc on the protagonist's homeland.

Mind Control
The antagonist has the ability to manipulate the thoughts or emotions of others, creating internal conflict and trust issues for the protagonist and love interest.

The antagonist uses their power to sow doubt and suspicion between the protagonist and the love interest, jeopardizing their relationship.

Shapeshifting
The antagonist can change their appearance or form, making them a difficult adversary to track and confront.

The antagonist takes on different guises to infiltrate the protagonist's inner circle, gathering information to use against them.

Immortality or Regeneration
The antagonist is difficult to defeat due to their ability to heal rapidly or escape death, making them a constant threat to the protagonist and love interest.

The antagonist can regenerate from any injury, forcing the protagonist to find a creative way to subdue them permanently.

Mastery of Dark Arts
The antagonist is skilled in forbidden magic or dark arts, using their knowledge to unleash powerful forces against the protagonist and love interest.

The antagonist summons demons or raises the dead to do their bidding, creating obstacles for the protagonist and love interest to overcome.

Flaws and Vulnerabilities
Give the antagonist flaws and vulnerabilities that make them more human and relatable. These imperfections can lead to internal conflicts within the antagonist or create opportunities for the protagonist to exploit in their struggle against them.

Overconfidence
The antagonist's arrogance can cause them to underestimate the protagonist, leading to mistakes or miscalculations.

The antagonist's overconfidence allows the protagonist to surprise them with an unexpected strategy or alliance, turning the tide of battle.

Obsession

The antagonist's fixation on a particular goal, person, or idea can cause them to become blind to potential threats or consequences.

The antagonist's obsession with the love interest leads them to neglect other aspects of their plan, creating opportunities for the protagonist to intervene.

Fear of Failure

The antagonist's fear of failing in their mission or losing their status can make them overly cautious or prone to self-sabotage.

The antagonist hesitates at a crucial moment, giving the protagonist the chance to gain the upper hand.

Guilt or Remorse

The antagonist's feelings of guilt or remorse for past actions can create internal conflict and moments of vulnerability.

The antagonist's guilt over a past misdeed makes them hesitate in their pursuit of the protagonist, providing an opportunity for redemption or change.

Uncontrolled Emotions

The antagonist's inability to control their emotions, such as anger or jealousy, can lead to impulsive decisions or cloud their judgment.

The antagonist's jealousy of the protagonist's relationship with the love interest causes them to act rashly, exposing a weakness in their defenses.

Loyalty or Love

The antagonist's loyalty to a particular person or group can create conflict between their personal feelings and their larger goals.

The antagonist's loyalty to a family member or friend makes them question their actions, potentially causing them to waver in their pursuit of the protagonist.

Insecurity

The antagonist's feelings of insecurity or self-doubt can undermine their confidence or make them susceptible to manipulation.

The protagonist exploits the antagonist's insecurities, causing them to question their actions and motives.

Personal Connection

Establish a personal connection between the antagonist and the protagonist or love interest. A personal connection can add emotional depth to their conflict and create opportunities for character growth and development.

Shared History

The antagonist and the protagonist or love interest have a shared past, such as being childhood friends or former allies.

The antagonist and protagonist were once close friends, but a betrayal or a major disagreement caused them to become enemies.

Rivalry

The antagonist and the protagonist or love interest are rivals, competing for the same goal, resources, or status.

The protagonist and antagonist both vie for the love interest's affection, leading to a romantic rivalry that fuels their animosity.

Family Ties

The antagonist is related to the protagonist or love interest, making their conflict a deeply personal family affair.

The antagonist is the estranged sibling of the love interest, and their actions are driven by a desire for revenge or reconciliation.

Unrequited Love

The antagonist has unrequited feelings for the protagonist or love interest, leading to jealousy, resentment, or obsession.

66

The antagonist loves the protagonist but is spurned, causing them to become a vengeful adversary.

Mentor/Student Relationship
The antagonist was once a mentor or teacher to the protagonist or love interest, creating a complex dynamic of respect and betrayal.

The antagonist was the protagonist's mentor, but a clash of values led them to part ways and become adversaries.

Shared Tragedy
The antagonist and the protagonist or love interest are connected through a shared tragedy or loss, leading to a mutual understanding or sympathy despite their conflict.

The protagonist and antagonist both lost loved ones in a devastating event, forging a complex bond between them even as they stand opposed.

Forced Alliance
The antagonist and the protagonist or love interest must work together, despite their animosity, to achieve a common goal or overcome a shared threat.

The protagonist and antagonist must join forces to defeat a greater evil, testing their ability to trust and cooperate with one another.

Dynamic Character
Allow the antagonist to change and grow throughout the story. They may learn from their mistakes, adapt to new challenges, or even experience a change of heart. Showing growth and development in the antagonist can make them a more compelling and nuanced character.

Redeeming Qualities
Throughout the story, reveal redeeming qualities or moments of kindness in the antagonist, making them a more complex and sympathetic character.

The antagonist shows unexpected compassion towards a vulnerable character, causing the protagonist and the reader to reevaluate their perception of them.

Self-Reflection
The antagonist begins to question their own motivations or actions, leading to internal conflict and potential changes in their behavior.

The antagonist starts to doubt the righteousness of their cause, leading them to reconsider their goals and alliances.

Learning From Mistakes
The antagonist recognizes their errors and takes steps to correct them, demonstrating their ability to grow and adapt.

After a significant defeat, the antagonist reevaluates their strategy and learns from their past mistakes, becoming a more formidable adversary.

Personal Growth
The antagonist overcomes their flaws or personal demons, evolving as a character and gaining the reader's respect.

The antagonist confronts their fear of failure or abandonment, allowing them to approach their goals with newfound determination and courage.

Relationship Development
The antagonist's relationships with other characters evolve and change, revealing new aspects of their personality and motivations.

The antagonist forms an unexpected friendship or alliance with a secondary character, showing their capacity for trust and loyalty.

Change of Heart
The antagonist experiences a significant event or revelation that leads to a change of heart, transforming their role in the story.

The antagonist discovers a hidden truth about their past or the consequences of their actions, prompting them to seek redemption or switch sides.

Sacrifice
The antagonist makes a personal sacrifice for the greater good or for the sake of a loved one, highlighting their capacity for selflessness and growth.

The antagonist sacrifices their own safety or power to protect an innocent or to aid the protagonist in a crucial moment.

Moral Complexity
Make the antagonist morally complex by providing them with valid reasons for their actions and beliefs. This can create moral dilemmas for the protagonist and love interest and challenge the reader's perception of right and wrong.

Noble Cause
The antagonist believes their actions serve a greater good, forcing the protagonist and love interest to question whether the ends justify the means.

The antagonist seeks to overthrow a corrupt regime, resorting to morally questionable tactics that put innocent lives at risk, leading the protagonist and love interest to struggle with their own beliefs.

Personal Tragedy
The antagonist's actions are fueled by a past trauma or personal loss, making their motivations more relatable and sympathetic.

The antagonist seeks revenge for the death of a loved one, causing the protagonist and love interest to empathize with their pain while grappling with the consequences of their actions.

Shared Goal
The antagonist shares a common goal with the protagonist and love interest but approaches it through different methods or beliefs, leading to moral and ethical debates.

Both the antagonist and the protagonist seek to protect their homeland, but the antagonist's methods are more ruthless and unforgiving, leading to moral conflict between the characters.

Gray Area

The antagonist operates within a moral gray area, where their actions may be neither entirely good nor entirely evil, forcing the protagonist and love interest to question their own moral compass.

The antagonist is a vigilante who takes justice into their own hands, using extreme measures to punish criminals, making the protagonist and love interest wrestle with the concept of vigilante justice.

Moral Redemption

The antagonist seeks redemption or forgiveness for past actions, making them a more complex and sympathetic character.

The antagonist attempts to atone for their past misdeeds by helping the protagonist and love interest, leading the characters to confront their own capacity for forgiveness and redemption.

Unintended Consequences

The antagonist's actions have unforeseen consequences, forcing the protagonist and love interest to weigh the potential costs and benefits of their actions.

The antagonist's efforts to create a utopian society inadvertently lead to suffering and oppression, causing the protagonist and love interest to question the viability of such an ideal.

The Side Characters

They serve to enhance the protagonist's journey, providing context, depth, and interest to the story. They can create tension and conflict, offer advice and support, and add an element of realism and relatability to the fantasy world.

These are characters who support the main characters and help move the story forward. They can be friends, family, or acquaintances, and should be interesting and well-rounded, providing humor, insight, or emotional support.

Distinct Personality

Give each side character a unique personality, with their own quirks, interests, and mannerisms. This will make them more memorable and add variety to the story.

The Jester

A side character who always has a witty remark or joke to lighten the mood, even in tense situations. They may use humor as a coping mechanism or to bring people together.

A bard who uses their musical talent to make people laugh and forget their troubles, providing comic relief during the heroes' journey.

The Loyal Friend

A side character who is unwaveringly loyal and protective of the protagonist or love interest. They may have a strong moral compass or a deep bond with the main characters.

A childhood friend of the protagonist who has always been there for them, offering support and encouragement throughout their adventures.

The Scholar

A side character who possesses vast knowledge and wisdom, often providing valuable insights or advice to the main characters. They may have a particular area of expertise, such as history, magic, or politics.

A wise old mage who aids the protagonist by offering guidance on magical matters and helps decipher ancient texts related to the story's central conflict.

The Free Spirit

A side character who is adventurous, spontaneous, and unafraid to take risks. They can inspire the main characters to step out of their comfort zones and embrace new experiences.

A wandering nomad who joins the protagonist's quest, teaching them to embrace the unpredictability of life and take chances.

The Dreamer

A side character who is idealistic and hopeful, often providing a sense of optimism and motivation to the main characters. They may have lofty goals or aspirations that inspire others.

A young aspiring knight who dreams of becoming a hero, inspiring the protagonist to believe in the power of hope and determination.

The Realist

A side character who is pragmatic and grounded, offering a counterbalance to the more idealistic or impulsive characters. They may help the main characters navigate difficult situations with a level-headed perspective.

A seasoned soldier who joins the protagonist's quest, offering strategic advice and practical solutions to problems the group encounters.

The Mysterious Stranger

A side character with a mysterious past or hidden agenda, creating intrigue and suspense. Their true motives may be revealed over time, adding complexity to the story.

A mysterious rogue who joins the protagonist's journey, gradually revealing their past and how it connects to the main plot.

Backstory

Provide side characters with a backstory that explains their motivations, beliefs, and past experiences. This will give them depth and make their actions more understandable to the reader.

Tragic Past

A side character experienced a tragedy or loss that shaped their beliefs and actions, making their motivations more relatable and understandable.

A skilled healer who lost a loved one due to a preventable illness, driving them to help others and prevent similar tragedies.

Personal Redemption
A side character is on a quest for redemption or forgiveness, making their actions more sympathetic and adding emotional depth.

A former thief seeking to make amends for their past actions by using their skills to help the protagonist and love interest on their journey.

Mentorship
A side character was influenced or mentored by a significant figure in their past, affecting their beliefs and motivations.

A warrior who was trained by a legendary hero, striving to live up to their mentor's expectations and uphold their values.

Unfulfilled Dreams
A side character had dreams or aspirations that were unfulfilled, driving their actions and decisions throughout the story.

A talented musician who was never able to achieve fame or recognition, joining the protagonist's quest in search of a new purpose and a chance to share their gift.

Family Legacy
A side character is motivated by their family's history or expectations, shaping their goals and actions in the story.

A noble's child who feels pressured to uphold their family's honor, leading them to make difficult choices that affect the protagonist and love interest.

Challenging Upbringing
A side character faced adversity or challenges in their past, influencing their outlook and motivations.

A side character who grew up in poverty, developing a strong sense of empathy and compassion for others in need, joining the protagonist's cause to make a difference in the world.

<u>Past Relationships</u>
A side character's past relationships, romantic or otherwise, can shape their beliefs, motivations, and actions in the story.

A side character who experienced heartbreak, making them cautious or guarded in matters of love, but ultimately helping the protagonist or love interest navigate their own romantic entanglements.

Goals and Motivations

Just like the main characters, side characters should have their own goals and motivations that drive their actions throughout the story. These goals can be connected to the main plot or serve as subplots that enrich the narrative.

<u>Personal Quest</u>
A side character has their own personal quest or mission, which can either complement or intersect with the main plot.

A side character searching for a lost family member, leading them to cross paths with the protagonist and love interest, and ultimately contributing to the resolution of the main conflict.

<u>Uncovering Secrets</u>
A side character is driven to uncover a hidden truth or solve a mystery, which can reveal crucial information related to the main plot.

A side character investigating a mysterious prophecy that foretells the protagonist's role in an upcoming battle, adding depth and intrigue to the story.

<u>Pursuit of Power</u>
A side character seeks power or influence, driving their actions and creating potential conflicts or alliances with the protagonist and love interest.

A side character competing for the position of a high-ranking official, whose political ambitions affect the story's main conflict and romance.

Redemption or Atonement
A side character is motivated by a desire for redemption or atonement for past wrongdoings, leading to personal growth and a subplot that supports the main narrative.

A side character who once betrayed the protagonist, seeking to regain their trust and make amends by helping them on their journey.

Rivalry or Competition
A side character has a rivalry or competition with another character, which can add tension or drama to the story and influence the main plot.

A side character vying for the love interest's affection, creating romantic tension and pushing the protagonist to confront their feelings.

Protecting a Loved One
A side character is motivated by the desire to protect a loved one, adding emotional depth and personal stakes to the narrative.

A side character determined to save their sibling from the antagonist's clutches, leading them to join forces with the protagonist and love interest in their quest.

Pursuit of Knowledge
A side character seeks knowledge or understanding, which can provide valuable insights or revelations that affect the main plot.

A side character researching ancient magic to find a way to defeat the antagonist, unearthing crucial information that aids the protagonist in their struggle.

Relationships

Develop the relationships between side characters and the main characters, as well as among the side characters themselves. Strong relationships can add emotional depth to the story and contribute to character development.

<u>Friendship</u>
Establish strong friendships between side characters and the main
characters, built on trust, loyalty, and shared experiences.

A side character who has been the protagonist's best friend since
childhood, providing support and encouragement throughout the
story.

<u>Mentorship</u>
Create a mentor-mentee relationship between a side character and
one of the main characters, highlighting the exchange of knowledge
and guidance.

A wise mage who takes the love interest under their wing, teaching
them powerful magic that aids in their journey.

<u>Rivalry</u>
Introduce a rivalry between side characters and main characters or
among side characters, creating tension and challenges.

A side character who constantly competes with the protagonist for
recognition, pushing both characters to grow and improve.

<u>Romantic Connections</u>
Explore romantic relationships between side characters and main
characters or among side characters, adding emotional depth and
complexity to the story.

A love triangle involving a side character, the protagonist, and the
love interest, which tests their bonds and forces them to confront
their feelings.

<u>Family Ties</u>
Establish familial connections between main characters and side
characters, highlighting the importance of family bonds and the
impact they have on the characters' decisions.

A side character who is the protagonist's sibling, with their
relationship playing a significant role in shaping their actions and
motivations.

<u>Alliance or Partnership</u>
Create alliances or partnerships between main characters and side characters or among side characters, emphasizing teamwork and cooperation.

A group of side characters who join forces with the protagonist and love interest to take down a common enemy, forming a strong bond in the process.

<u>Betrayal or Deception</u>
Introduce betrayal or deception in relationships between main characters and side characters or among side characters, adding drama and conflict to the story.

A side character who secretly works for the antagonist, ultimately betraying the protagonist's trust and forcing them to reevaluate their relationships.

Character Arc

Allow side characters to grow and change over the course of the story.

<u>Personal Growth</u>
Show side characters overcoming personal obstacles or fears, demonstrating their growth and development.

A timid side character who, throughout the story, gains confidence and courage, eventually standing up for themselves in a crucial moment.

<u>Learning From Mistakes</u>
Have side characters learn from their mistakes, showing their ability to adapt and evolve.

A side character who initially betrays the protagonist, but later realizes their error and seeks redemption by helping the protagonist and love interest.

Changing Relationships

Develop the relationships between side characters and main characters or among side characters, reflecting their growth and shifting dynamics.

A side character who starts off as a rival to the protagonist, but gradually becomes an ally as they learn to respect and understand each other.

New Skills or Abilities

Allow side characters to acquire new skills or abilities, demonstrating their growth and expanding their role in the story.

A side character who initially struggles with magic, but through dedication and practice, becomes a powerful mage, contributing to the resolution of the main conflict.

Changes in Beliefs or Values

Show side characters reevaluating their beliefs or values as a result of their experiences in the story, highlighting their growth and development.

A side character who initially supports the antagonist's cause but, after witnessing their cruelty, decides to change sides and fight for justice.

Accepting Responsibility

Have side characters accept responsibility for their actions, demonstrating their maturity and growth.

A side character who initially avoids responsibility for their actions, but eventually owns up to their mistakes and makes amends with those they've hurt.

Sacrifice

Show side characters making sacrifices or enduring personal loss for the greater good or to protect the main characters, highlighting their growth and commitment.

A side character who willingly sacrifices their own safety to ensure
the success of the protagonist's mission, demonstrating their
selflessness and growth.

Purpose in the Story

Ensure that each side character serves a purpose in the story. This
will make them feel integral to the narrative and prevent them from
feeling like mere background fillers.

Comic Relief

Include side characters that lighten the mood and provide humor,
offering readers a break from the story's tension.

A witty side character who frequently cracks jokes and engages in
banter with the main characters, helping to break up intense
moments.

Advice and Guidance

Have side characters who offer insights, wisdom, or advice to the
main characters, helping them navigate challenges or make
decisions.

An elder side character who has experienced similar struggles and
shares their wisdom with the protagonist, guiding them through
difficult situations.

Emotional Support

Include side characters that provide emotional support to the main
characters, helping them cope with personal struggles and
emotional challenges.

A loyal friend who is always there to listen and offer a shoulder to
cry on for the protagonist during difficult times.

Key Role in the Plot

Ensure some side characters play essential roles in the progression
of the plot or resolution of the conflict.

A side character who possesses a unique skill or ability that
ultimately becomes crucial to the success of the main characters'
mission.

<u>Moral Compass</u>
Have side characters who challenge the main characters' beliefs or actions, encouraging them to reflect on their choices and values.

A side character who constantly questions the protagonist's decisions, forcing them to reevaluate their actions and consider the consequences.

<u>Foil</u>
Use side characters as foils to the main characters, highlighting their strengths or weaknesses and adding depth to the narrative.

A side character who is the polar opposite of the protagonist, emphasizing the protagonist's unique qualities and strengths.

<u>Catalyst for Change</u>
Include side characters that serve as catalysts for the main characters' growth or development, pushing them to change and evolve.

A side character who confronts the protagonist about their flaws or mistakes, ultimately leading the protagonist to grow and change for the better.

Flaws and Vulnerabilities

Give side characters their own flaws and vulnerabilities, making them more relatable and human. This can create opportunities for character growth and add depth to their interactions with the main characters.

<u>Personal Fears or Insecurities</u>
Give side characters their own fears or insecurities that they must confront or overcome throughout the story.

A side character who is afraid of the dark, facing their fear when venturing into a dangerous, dark cavern with the main characters.

<u>Past Traumas or Regrets</u>
Provide side characters with past experiences that continue to affect them, shaping their beliefs or actions.

A side character who lost a loved one in a tragic accident, struggling to cope with their grief and learning to find closure with the help of the main characters.

Conflicting Desires or Loyalties
Create side characters with conflicting desires or loyalties, forcing them to make difficult decisions and face the consequences.

A side character torn between their loyalty to their family and their newfound friendship with the protagonist, ultimately choosing to follow their own moral compass.

Mistakes and Failures
Allow side characters to make mistakes or experience failure, showing their growth as they learn from these experiences.

A side character who inadvertently betrays the protagonist's trust but later earns their forgiveness by proving their loyalty and dedication to the cause.

Flawed Beliefs or Values
Give side characters flawed beliefs or values that they must reevaluate over the course of the story.

A side character who initially holds prejudiced beliefs about a particular group but learns to recognize and overcome their biases through their interactions with the main characters.

Limited Skills or Abilities
Provide side characters with limitations in their skills or abilities, making them more relatable and human.

A side character who is a skilled healer but struggles with combat, learning to develop their fighting skills and finding courage in the face of danger.

Personal Obstacles or Challenges
Create side characters who face personal obstacles or challenges that they must overcome to grow and develop.

A side character who is struggling with addiction, confronting their problem with the support of the main characters and finding the strength to change.

Balancing Screen Time

Distribute "screen time" or focus among side characters, ensuring that each has a chance to shine and contribute to the story. Be careful not to overcrowd the narrative with too many side characters, as this can dilute the impact of each character and make the story feel cluttered.

Rotate Focus

Shift the focus between side characters in different scenes or chapters, allowing each character to have their moments and make meaningful contributions to the story.

Dedicate a chapter to a side character's backstory or personal journey, revealing their motivations and how they connect to the main plot.

Subplots

Create subplots that center around side characters, giving them a chance to develop and showcase their unique traits and abilities.

A side character tasked with solving a mystery or overcoming a personal challenge that runs parallel to the main plot.

Pairings or Groups

Pair side characters with the main characters or other side characters, allowing them to interact, develop relationships, and reveal their strengths and weaknesses.

Have a side character team up with the protagonist on a dangerous mission, showcasing their unique skills and deepening their bond.

Character Arcs

Develop individual character arcs for side characters that intersect with the main plot, providing opportunities for growth and development.

A side character who starts as an antagonist but gradually becomes an ally to the protagonist, experiencing redemption and personal growth.

Key Moments

Give side characters key moments in the story where their actions or decisions have a significant impact on the main plot or characters.

A side character who makes a crucial discovery or sacrifices themselves to save the protagonist, highlighting their importance to the story.

Dynamic Relationships

Develop dynamic relationships between side characters and the main characters, allowing each side character to play a meaningful role in the protagonist's or love interest's journey.

A side character who serves as a mentor, friend, or rival to the protagonist, pushing them to grow and evolve.

Balancing Ensembles

In stories with an ensemble cast, balance the focus between side characters by ensuring that each has a distinct role and contributes to the group's dynamic.

A group of side characters that each bring unique skills, perspectives, and personalities to the team, working together to overcome challenges and achieve their goals.

World-Specific Characters

These characters help to create a sense of wonder and excitement, transporting readers to a world that is vastly different from our own. They can add an element of magic and whimsy to the story, while also serving to drive the plot and themes forward.

In a fantasy setting, you may have mythical creatures, magical beings, or other unique characters that are specific to the world you've created. These characters can add depth and intrigue to your story.

Consider the World's Unique Aspects

Consider the specific elements of your fantasy world, such as its history, culture, geography, magic systems, or politics, and use them to inform the backgrounds and traits of your characters.

Unique Races or Species

Introduce races or species that are unique to your fantasy world, with distinct appearances, abilities, and cultural practices. This can add depth and intrigue to your story, offering readers a glimpse into a world different from our own.

A race of winged beings who live in sky cities and possess the ability to control the wind.

Magic Users or Supernatural Beings

Incorporate characters with magical abilities or supernatural origins, showcasing the wonder and power of your fantasy world.

A character who can manipulate elements, such as fire or water, or a character who is part of a secret order of magical protectors.

Distinctive Occupations or Roles

Create characters with occupations or roles that are unique to your fantasy world, reflecting its culture, politics, or social structure.

A character who works as a memory merchant, buying and selling memories in a world where such transactions are commonplace.

Cultural Customs and Traditions

Develop characters that embody the customs, traditions, or beliefs of their culture, showcasing the rich diversity and history of your fantasy world.

A character from a society that values storytelling and oral history, with a unique ability to recount tales of the past through song or dance.

Unique Appearance or Fashion

Give your characters distinctive appearances or styles that reflect the aesthetics, materials, and fashion of your fantasy world.

A character who wears intricate and colorful garments made from the feathers of a rare, magical bird.

Language and Dialects

Incorporate unique languages, dialects, or slang into your characters' speech, adding depth and authenticity to your fantasy world.

A character who speaks a distinct dialect that reflects their regional background, using words or phrases that are unique to their culture.

Mythology and Folklore

Develop characters that are part of or influenced by the mythology and folklore of your fantasy world, enriching your story with a sense of history and wonder.

A character who is a descendant of a legendary hero, or one who is on a quest to fulfill an ancient prophecy.

Define Cultural and Social Norms

Develop cultural and social norms for different regions or groups in your world. Consider how these norms influence your characters' behavior, values, customs, clothing, and language.

Desert Region

Where water is scarce and precious, a character might value resourcefulness, endurance, and adaptability. They could have a unique way of expressing affection by offering their partner a sip from their water skin, a symbol of trust and commitment.

Isolated Village

A character might have a strong sense of community and tradition, which could lead to conflict with a love interest from a more cosmopolitan and individualistic background. They might have a custom of exchanging intricately carved wooden tokens as a sign of commitment in a romantic relationship.

Strong Belief in Fate and Destiny

A character might struggle to accept their growing feelings for someone who doesn't share the same beliefs. They could have a ritual where couples read each other's palms or consult an oracle to determine if they are destined to be together.

Strict Gender Rules

A character might find it difficult to navigate a romance with someone who challenges these norms. A female warrior from a matriarchal society might be intrigued by a male character from a more egalitarian culture, leading to a clash of expectations and values.

Rich History of Magic and Sorcery

A character might use unique spells or enchantments in their courtship, such as sending magically encoded love letters that only their intended can read or conjuring a romantic dinner under a starry sky.

Values art and Creativity

A character might express their feelings through poetry, music, or dance. Their courtship rituals could involve composing songs or poems for their love interest or participating in elaborate dance performances to showcase their devotion.

Strict Caste System

A character might be drawn to someone from a different social class, creating tension and conflict as they navigate the expectations and prejudices of their world. They might have a secret code or gesture to communicate their love and support for each other without drawing attention.

Develop Diverse Backgrounds

Create characters with diverse backgrounds, coming from different social classes, professions, or regions of your fantasy world. This will add variety to your cast and allow for interesting interactions and conflicts.

Nobility & Commoners

A noble character visiting a local market might encounter a resourceful street vendor, leading to a clash of values and expectations, or perhaps an unexpected friendship.

<u>Different Magical Abilities</u>
A character with the power to heal might cross paths with a character who can manipulate time, resulting in a unique collaboration to solve a problem or overcome a challenge.

<u>Skilled Trades & Craftsmen</u>
A blacksmith renowned for crafting magical weapons might be sought after by an enigmatic character who needs a unique artifact, sparking intrigue and suspicion.

<u>Scholarly & Adventurous Characters</u>
A studious historian with extensive knowledge of ancient civilizations might join forces with a daring explorer to uncover lost artifacts or decipher ancient texts.

<u>Warriors & Pacifists</u>
A skilled warrior who is loyal to their kingdom might have a tense encounter with a pacifist from a neighboring nation, leading to a heated debate or an opportunity to learn from one another.

<u>Religious & Secular Characters</u>
A devout priestess devoted to a specific deity might interact with a skeptical character who challenges her beliefs, resulting in philosophical discussions or a clash of worldviews.

<u>Diverse Regional Backgrounds</u>
A character hailing from a lush forest region might be fascinated by a character from a vast desert, sparking curiosity and cultural exchange as they learn about each other's customs and ways of life.

Incorporate Magic or Supernatural Elements
If your world includes magic or supernatural elements, consider how these aspects might shape your characters.

<u>Magical Abilities</u>
A character who can communicate with animals might serve as a liaison between the human and animal kingdoms, helping to maintain balance and understanding between the two.

Magical Races
A shapeshifter from a secluded community might struggle with the prejudice and fear of others while trying to integrate into the larger world, leading to a storyline about acceptance and understanding.

Impacted by Magical Events
A character who lost their home due to a magical catastrophe might become an advocate for magical regulations or a leader in rebuilding efforts, bringing a personal perspective to the consequences of magical events.

Magical Artisans
A skilled weaver with the ability to imbue garments with protective or enchanting properties might provide essential support to characters on their quest or become a sought-after figure in their community.

Magical Creatures
A character who is a caretaker for mythical beasts, such as griffins or unicorns, might be involved in preserving the natural habitats and protecting these creatures from potential harm or exploitation.

Magical Institutions
A character who works in a magical library or academy might be an invaluable resource for the protagonists, offering guidance and information about the supernatural elements they encounter.

Magical Healers
A character who has the power to heal others using magical plants and potions might serve as a crucial support to the community, using their abilities to mend wounds and cure ailments that cannot be addressed by conventional means.

Create Unique Professions or Roles

Design unique professions or roles that are specific to your fantasy world and assign them to your characters. This can help to emphasize the distinct nature of your setting and showcase the characters' skills and expertise.

Consider Your World's Culture and Environment
Think about the unique aspects of your fantasy world, such as its
geography, resources, technology, magic system, and social
dynamics. These elements can influence the development of
specialized professions or roles.

In a world where magic crystals power various technologies, a
Crystal Crafter might be responsible for crafting and refining these
crystals to suit different purposes.

Identify Gaps or Niches in Your World
Look for areas where a unique profession or role would fill a need
or solve a problem within your world. This can help you come up
with creative occupations that are specific to your setting.

In a world with dangerous, enchanted forests, you might have
Wayfinders who are experts in navigating and warding off the
magical threats within these forests.

Combine Existing Professions or Roles
You can create new and unique professions by merging or
modifying existing ones, adjusting them to fit your world's specific
conditions or challenges.

In a world where people can communicate with animals, a Beast
Diplomat could be responsible for maintaining relations between
humans and various animal species.

Focus On the Skills and Expertise
Ensure that the unique professions you create showcase the
characters' skills and expertise, making them valuable contributors
to the story.

A Dreamweaver might be an expert in entering and manipulating
people's dreams, using this ability to provide valuable insights or
guidance to the main characters.

Reflect On How These Professions Interact with Other Characters
Consider how the unique professions or roles will interact with the
main characters, love interest, mentors, antagonists, and side

characters. This can create interesting dynamics and enrich the
relationships between characters.

A character who is an Aetherial Dancer might use their knowledge
of a unique, magical dance form to teach the protagonist and love
interest a new way to communicate their emotions, deepening their
bond.

Use World-Specific Character Arcs

Craft character arcs that are influenced by the events, conflicts, and
themes of your fantasy world. This will help to integrate your
characters into the larger narrative and make their stories feel more
grounded in the world.

Identify Relevant Events and Conflicts
Consider the major events, conflicts, and themes of your fantasy
world, and think about how they might impact or involve your
world-specific characters.

In a world where two kingdoms are at war over magical resources, a
Crystal Crafter might be caught in the conflict as both sides try to
secure their expertise.

Define the Character's Initial State
Establish the starting point for each world-specific character,
considering their background, beliefs, goals, and relationships. This
initial state will set the stage for the character's growth and
development.

The Crystal Crafter is initially neutral, focusing solely on their craft
and avoiding involvement in the conflict.

Identify Challenges and Turning Points
Determine key challenges or turning points that will force the
character to confront the events, conflicts, and themes of your
world. These moments can push the character to change or adapt,
driving their arc forward.

The Crystal Crafter's workshop is destroyed in an attack, forcing
them to confront the reality of the war and make a choice about
their role in it.

92

Show the Character's Growth and Development
As your world-specific characters face these challenges and turning points, demonstrate their growth and development, whether it be a change in beliefs, goals, relationships, or actions.

The Crystal Crafter decides to use their skills to create a powerful artifact that can help end the war and bring peace to the land.

Reach A Resolution or Transformation
Conclude the character arc with a resolution or transformation that reflects the character's growth and development, showing how they have been affected by the events, conflicts, and themes of your world.

The Crystal Crafter successfully creates the artifact, and in the process, learns the value of using their skills for the greater good, committing to aid others in the future.

Connect the Character's Arc to the Larger Narrative
Ensure that the character's arc is intertwined with the main plot or other characters' storylines, reinforcing the connection between the world-specific characters and the larger narrative.

The protagonist, who is involved in the war, encounters the Crystal Crafter and helps them complete their goal, creating a bond between the characters and further integrating the world-specific character into the main story.

Design Distinctive Character Appearances
Give your characters appearances that reflect the world they inhabit, incorporating elements like clothing, accessories, or physical traits that are unique to your fantasy setting.

Consider The Environment and Climate
Consider the environment and climate of your fantasy world when designing your characters' appearances. This can include factors like temperature, weather, and terrain.

In a desert region, characters might wear loose, light clothing and head coverings to protect themselves from the sun and sand.

Reflect the Region's Resources and Materials
Incorporate materials and resources that are unique to, or abundant in, different regions of your world. This can influence clothing, accessories, and even physical traits.

A character from a volcanic region might wear clothing made from a fire-resistant fabric derived from a local plant and have ash-gray hair due to generations of exposure to volcanic ash.

Incorporate Cultural and Social Influences
Consider the cultural and social influences of your world when designing your characters' appearances. This can include aspects like fashion, social status, and religious or spiritual beliefs.

In a society where social status is determined by one's magical ability, characters might wear accessories that display their magical prowess, such as enchanted amulets or gemstones that glow with power.

Use Unique Physical Traits or Features
Incorporate unique physical traits or features that are specific to your fantasy world or certain regions within it. These traits can be influenced by factors such as genetics, magic, or the environment.

Characters from a region near a magical vortex might have unusual eye colors or patterns, like swirling irises or star-like pupils, as a result of prolonged exposure to magical energies.

Integrate Elements of Your World's Magic or Technology
If your world has unique magical or technological elements, consider incorporating them into your characters' appearances in the form of clothing, accessories, or physical traits.

In a world with advanced clockwork technology, a character might have a prosthetic limb made of intricate gears and cogs.

Create Visual Consistency Within Groups or Regions
Ensure that characters from the same region or cultural group share some visual elements or traits, creating a sense of consistency and cohesion within your world.

Characters from a nomadic tribe might all wear distinctive embroidered patterns on their clothing, signifying their shared heritage and traditions.

Use World-Specific Conflicts and Challenges

Introduce conflicts and challenges that are specific to your fantasy world and its unique features. This can help to test your characters' abilities, force them to adapt, and reveal their true nature.

Identify Unique Features of Your World
Consider the unique features of your fantasy world, such as its environment, magic system, technology, social dynamics, or history.

In a world where a rare magical resource is running out, conflicts might arise over the control, distribution, or use of this resource.

Create Conflicts Based on The Characters' Roles or Professions
Design conflicts and challenges that stem from the world-specific characters' roles or professions within your fantasy world, testing their skills and expertise.

A Dreamweaver might face a challenge when a powerful entity starts corrupting people's dreams, forcing them to confront their own fears and limitations in order to save others.

Incorporate Interpersonal and Cultural Conflicts
Introduce conflicts and challenges that arise from differences in culture, beliefs, or values among characters or groups in your world, leading to misunderstandings or clashes.

A Beast Diplomat might struggle to mediate a dispute between humans and a previously unknown species, facing cultural barriers and mistrust from both sides.

Utilize Environmental or External Challenges
Create conflicts and challenges that arise from the environment or external factors in your world, forcing characters to adapt or overcome obstacles.

A Wayfinder leading a group through an enchanted forest might encounter a magical storm that alters the landscape, testing their navigation skills and resourcefulness.

Integrate Conflicts and Challenges into The Main Plot
Ensure that the conflicts and challenges faced by world-specific characters are connected to the main plot or other characters' storylines, integrating them into the larger narrative.

The protagonist, who is involved in the quest for the rare magical resource, encounters the Dreamweaver during their journey, and together they must confront the powerful entity causing corruption.

Show The Characters' Growth and True Nature
As your world-specific characters face these conflicts and challenges, reveal their true nature, showcasing their strengths, weaknesses, and personal growth.

The Beast Diplomat, after overcoming the mistrust and cultural barriers, demonstrates their compassion, patience, and diplomacy, ultimately finding a solution to the dispute that benefits both parties.

Develop Relationships Based on The World's Unique Aspects

Create relationships between your characters that are influenced by the specific elements of your fantasy world, such as political alliances, cultural differences, or magical connections.

Use Political Alliances and Rivalries
Craft relationships between characters that are shaped by political alliances or rivalries in your world, highlighting the influence of power dynamics and the struggle for influence.

A character from a powerful noble family might have a strained relationship with a character from a rival family, with their interactions marked by suspicion and intrigue.

Incorporate Cultural Differences
Develop relationships between characters from different cultures, allowing for misunderstandings, growth, and the bridging of cultural gaps.

A character from a matriarchal society might initially clash with a character from a patriarchal society, but through their interactions, they learn to understand and appreciate each other's perspectives and values.

Explore Magical Connections or Bonds
Create relationships between characters that are influenced by magical connections or bonds, showcasing the impact of magic on personal connections and emotions.

Two characters might share a magical bond that allows them to sense each other's emotions, leading to a deep understanding and trust that transcends cultural or political differences.

Utilize Shared Goals or Interests
Develop relationships between characters that are formed by their shared goals or interests, highlighting the ways that common pursuits can bring people together in your world.

Characters from different factions might form an unlikely alliance to protect a sacred site from destruction, building a bond of friendship and trust through their shared purpose.

Integrate Social Dynamics and Class Differences
Craft relationships between characters that are shaped by the social dynamics and class differences in your world, exploring the impact of these factors on personal connections.

A character from a lower social class might have a complex relationship with a character from a higher class, with their interactions revealing the challenges and tensions that arise from their different social standings.

<u>Employ Mentorship or Apprenticeship Roles</u>
Create relationships between characters that involve mentorship or apprenticeship, allowing for the exploration of personal growth, learning, and the passing down of knowledge and skills.

A skilled warrior might take on a young character from a different culture as an apprentice, fostering a bond that transcends their differences as they learn from one another.

Showcase The World Through Characters' Perspectives

Use your characters' perspectives to reveal different aspects of your fantasy world, such as its history, customs, beliefs, or magical systems. This can help to create a more immersive and vivid setting for your readers.

<u>Scholarly Perspective</u>
An erudite scholar can offer insights into the world's history and magical systems. They might reference ancient texts, discuss theories about the origins of magic, or recount historical events, thereby educating both other characters and readers about the world's backstory.

<u>Artisan Perspective</u>
A character who's an artisan, like a blacksmith or a weaver, can offer insights into the everyday customs and technologies of the world. They might discuss local trade practices, regional variations in craft techniques, or how magical enchantments are incorporated into their work, thereby bringing the world's everyday details to life.

<u>Religious Leader's Perspective</u>
A priest or priestess can reveal the world's religious beliefs and spiritual practices. They might discuss the pantheon of gods, perform sacred rituals, or interpret divine omens, thereby deepening the world's spiritual complexity.

<u>Outsider's Perspective</u>
A foreigner or an outcast can offer a unique viewpoint on the world's customs and values. They might question local traditions, struggle to understand the magic system, or comment on societal norms from an outsider's perspective, thereby highlighting cultural differences within the world.

98

<u>Magical Creature's Perspective</u>
A magical creature, like a dragon or a fairy, can shed light on the world's magical creatures and their unique abilities. They might share stories about their species, demonstrate their magical powers, or explain their relationship with humans, thereby enriching the world's fantastical elements.

Character Interactions

The Protagonist
&
The Love Interest

The Protagonist and The Love Interest Meeting

Magical Artifact

The protagonist discovers a magical artifact that accidentally summons the love interest from another realm or time. As they work together to solve the mystery of the artifact, they find themselves drawn to each other.

Quest

The protagonist is sent on a quest by a powerful figure or deity, and along the journey, they encounter the love interest, who is also on a mission. Together, they face challenges and grow closer.

Prophecy

A prophecy foretells that the protagonist and the love interest are destined to be together, but they initially reject the idea. They meet during a royal or religious ceremony and are forced to confront their feelings as they're thrown into a life-changing adventure.

Shapeshifter

The love interest is a shapeshifter who saves the protagonist from a dangerous situation while in their animal form. Later, they meet in their human form and develop a romantic connection.

Magical School

Both the protagonist and the love interest attend a magical school or academy, where they become partners in a class project or competition, allowing their relationship to blossom.

Hidden Identity

The protagonist is of royal or noble lineage but is hiding their identity. They meet the love interest, who belongs to a rival kingdom or faction, and fall in love without knowing each other's true background.

Familiar

The love interest is initially a magical creature (such as a fairy or dragon) that serves as the protagonist's familiar. They later gain the ability to transform into a human, allowing a romance to develop.

Cursed Lovers

The protagonist and the love interest are cursed lovers who are reborn in different time periods or realms, destined to find and lose each other repeatedly. They meet again in the story's present timeline and work together to break the curse.

Magical Tournament

The protagonist and the love interest are competitors in a magical tournament, where they initially view each other as rivals but eventually form a bond and fall in love.

Dream Connections

The protagonist and the love interest share a telepathic or dream connection, allowing them to communicate and grow close without physically meeting. When they finally meet in person, their bond strengthens, and romance blossoms.

What if the Characters Already Know Each Other?

Reunion

The protagonist and the love interest have been separated for some time, and the story opens with their long-awaited reunion, sparking a rekindling of their feelings for each other.

Sparring Session

The protagonist and the love interest share a friendly rivalry, and their first scene together features a sparring session or magical duel, highlighting their chemistry and competitive nature.

Collaborative Mission

The protagonist and the love interest are assigned a mission or task by their leader or mentor, and their first scene together involves them planning or strategizing, revealing their shared history and camaraderie.

Unexpected Encounter

The protagonist and the love interest unexpectedly cross paths in a magical market, tavern, or at a royal event, leading to a conversation that reestablishes their connection and possibly hints at romantic tension.

Saving Each Other

The protagonist and the love interest find themselves in a dangerous situation and must work together to save each other, highlighting their trust and mutual support.

Celebrating an Achievement

The protagonist and the love interest attend a celebration for a shared friend or family member's achievement, showcasing their pre-existing bond and providing an opportunity for their feelings to evolve.

Group Adventure

The protagonist and the love interest are part of a group of friends or allies embarking on an adventure or quest. Their first scene together reveals their roles within the group and sets the stage for their romance to develop further.

Secret Meetings

The protagonist and the love interest share a secret friendship or romance, and their first scene together shows them meeting clandestinely to exchange information, discuss their feelings, or share a stolen moment.

Childhood Flashback

The story starts with a flashback of the protagonist and the love interest as children, depicting a significant moment in their shared past that has shaped their current relationship.

Performing a Ritual

The protagonist and the love interest are tasked with performing a magical ritual or ceremony together, showcasing their compatibility and hinting at a deeper connection that could evolve into romance.

How Can the Characters Spend Time Together?

Magical Lessons

The protagonist and the love interest teach each other different magical skills or share knowledge about their respective magical backgrounds, allowing them to bond over their shared interests.

Joint Quests

The protagonist and the love interest embark on a series of quests or missions together, overcoming obstacles and facing challenges that strengthen their bond and understanding of each other.

Training Sessions

The protagonist and the love interest engage in training sessions or sparring matches, sharing tips and techniques while learning about each other's strengths and weaknesses.

Exploring Enchanted Places

The protagonist and the love interest explore enchanted forests, hidden caves, or magical cities together, discovering the wonders of their world and deepening their connection.

Solving Mysteries

The protagonist and the love interest work together to solve a magical mystery or decipher an ancient prophecy, using their combined knowledge and intuition to uncover the truth.

Potion Making

The protagonist and the love interest collaborate on brewing potions or concocting magical elixirs, showcasing their teamwork and intellectual compatibility.

Attending Magical Events

The protagonist and the love interest attend magical tournaments, festivals, or other events together, bonding over shared experiences and building a stronger connection.

Stargazing and Astrology

The protagonist and the love interest study the stars and celestial bodies together, discussing astrology and the impact of the cosmos on their magical world, allowing for deeper conversations and emotional intimacy.

Magical Creatures

The protagonist and the love interest share a mutual love for magical creatures and spend time together caring for or studying these beings, fostering a shared sense of purpose and compassion.

<u>Sharing Personal Stories</u>
The protagonist and the love interest take turns sharing personal stories or recounting their past experiences, including their families, childhood, and previous adventures, allowing them to understand each other on a deeper level and develop trust.

The Protagonist
&
The Sidekick

The Protagonist and The Sidekick Meeting

Accidental Encounter

The protagonist stumbles upon the sidekick in an unexpected situation, such as finding them trapped in a magical artifact, lost in a mystical forest, or hiding from a dangerous creature.

Common Adversary

The protagonist and the sidekick first cross paths while independently trying to defeat a common adversary. They might realize they can accomplish more by working together, leading to a partnership.

Rescue Mission

The protagonist saves or is saved by the sidekick during a conflict or dangerous situation. This shared experience creates an immediate bond between them.

Arranged Partnership

A higher authority or mutual mentor assigns the sidekick to aid the protagonist in their quest. This can create initial tension if the protagonist is resistant to the idea of needing help.

Mutual Quest

The protagonist and the sidekick meet when they are both set on the same quest, perhaps by a prophecy or a royal decree. They decide to embark on the journey together, realizing two heads are better than one.

Barter or Trade

The sidekick has a crucial piece of information or a unique skill that the protagonist needs. The protagonist may initially seek out the sidekick for this purpose, but their relationship grows over time.

Hidden Identity

The sidekick could initially hide their identity, posing as a simple stranger, only to reveal themselves when the time is right, creating an element of surprise.

<u>Familial or Childhood Connection</u>
The sidekick could be a childhood friend or a sibling of the protagonist who has always been there, but steps into the 'sidekick' role when the protagonist embarks on their quest.

<u>Forced Circumstances</u>
The protagonist and the sidekick could meet under forced circumstances, such as being imprisoned together and having to work together to escape.

<u>Prophetic Encounter</u>
A prophecy could foretell that the protagonist and the sidekick are destined to meet and work together. The moment they meet could be filled with anticipation and significance.

What if the Characters Already Know Each Other?

<u>Shared Ritual</u>
The protagonist and the sidekick could be introduced participating in a shared ritual or tradition, such as a magical practice or a customary game, highlighting their close bond and familiarity.

<u>Training Session</u>
The two could be engaged in a training session, showcasing their rapport, mutual trust, and the dynamics of their relationship. This could involve combat training, magical lessons, or strategy planning.

<u>Friendly Banter</u>
The protagonist and sidekick might be introduced in the middle of a friendly argument or banter, immediately demonstrating their camaraderie and the depth of their friendship.

<u>Mutual Task</u>
The protagonist and the sidekick could be working on a shared task, such as preparing for a journey, fixing a magical artifact, or researching a prophecy, showing their teamwork and shared commitment.

<u>Public Gathering</u>
They could first appear together at a public gathering, such as a festival or tournament, interacting with each other in a way that makes their relationship apparent to the reader.

<u>In the Midst of Action</u>
Their introduction could occur during an action sequence, where they are working together to overcome a challenge or defeat an enemy, demonstrating their partnership and reliance on each other.

<u>Emotional Support</u>
The protagonist could be seen seeking emotional support or advice from the sidekick after a tough situation, indicating their close emotional bond and the sidekick's role as a confidant.

<u>Familiar Environment</u>
The protagonist and the sidekick might be shown in a familiar place to them, like a shared home, a favorite hideout, or a secret meeting spot, signaling their shared history.

<u>Rescuing Each Other</u>
They could be introduced in a situation where they're rescuing each other from a sticky situation, showing their willingness to always have each other's backs.

<u>Teasing or Pranks</u>
The first scene could involve the protagonist and the sidekick engaged in a light-hearted prank or teasing each other, revealing their playful relationship and deep bond.

How Can the Characters Spend Time Together?

<u>Training Together</u>
The protagonist and the sidekick spend time honing their magical abilities or combat skills together. These sessions could lead to deeper conversations, shared struggles, and victories that help them understand each other better.

<u>Going on Mini Quests</u>
Before the main quest, the protagonist and the sidekick could go on smaller adventures or missions together, which can serve as

bonding experiences and reveal more about their personalities, strengths, and weaknesses.

Shared Hobbies or Interests

The protagonist and the sidekick could have shared hobbies or interests, such as playing a magical game, collecting mystical artifacts, or studying ancient lore, providing opportunities for them to spend time together outside their main quest.

Campfire Conversations

During their journey, they could have deep conversations by the campfire, sharing personal stories, fears, dreams, and aspirations, leading to greater understanding and intimacy.

Encountering Magical Creatures

They could spend time together interacting with magical creatures, either as a part of their quest or as a shared interest, leading to fun, adventurous, and bonding moments.

Navigating Enchanted Landscapes

The protagonist and the sidekick could explore enchanted forests, climb magical mountains, or sail mystical seas together. These shared experiences can facilitate bonding and provide opportunities for them to rely on and learn from each other.

Solving Mysteries or Puzzles

They could work together to solve magical puzzles or mysteries, which could help them learn more about each other's problem-solving approaches, creativity, and thought processes.

Overcoming Obstacles

Facing and overcoming challenges or obstacles together, such as escaping traps or outsmarting enemies, can strengthen their bond and reveal more about their characters.

Relaxing in Magical Settings

They could spend time together in magical settings, such as enchanted gardens, mystical waterfalls, or magical hot springs, providing relaxed environments for them to unwind and converse.

<u>Celebrating Victories</u>
They could celebrate their victories or achievements together, whether big or small, providing opportunities for them to express gratitude, admiration, and respect for each other.

The Protagonist
&
The Mentor

The Protagonist and The Mentor Meeting

Seeking Wisdom

The protagonist seeks out the mentor, a wise and experienced figure, to help them learn magic, control their newfound powers, or uncover the truth about their past or destiny.

Saving the Mentor

The protagonist inadvertently saves the mentor from a dangerous situation, such as an attack by dark forces or magical creatures. In gratitude, the mentor offers guidance and support to the protagonist.

Unexpected Encounter

The protagonist stumbles upon the mentor while exploring a hidden library, a mystical cave, or an enchanted forest. The mentor, sensing the protagonist's potential, decides to take them under their wing.

Royal Appointment

The protagonist is of noble or royal lineage and is assigned a mentor by the king or queen to help them develop their magical abilities, learn diplomacy, or prepare for a significant event.

Magical School

Both the protagonist and the mentor attend or teach at a magical school or academy, where the mentor takes a particular interest in the protagonist's education and growth.

Prophecy

A prophecy foretells that the protagonist will play a crucial role in the future of their world. The mentor, aware of the prophecy, seeks out the protagonist to train and prepare them for their destiny.

Family Connection

The mentor is a close friend or relative of the protagonist's family and has been entrusted with the responsibility of guiding and training the protagonist.

<u>Cursed Mentor</u>
The mentor is under a curse or magical affliction that the protagonist can help lift. As they work together to break the curse, the mentor shares their wisdom and experience with the protagonist.

<u>Chosen by a Deity</u>
The protagonist is chosen by a deity or supernatural being to fulfill a particular purpose. The deity sends the mentor to guide the protagonist on their journey and help them achieve their goals.

<u>Passing the Torch</u>
The mentor, nearing the end of their life or career, recognizes the potential in the protagonist and decides to pass on their knowledge, skills, and experiences to ensure the protagonist is prepared for the challenges ahead.

What if the Characters Already Know Each Other?

<u>Training Session</u>
The protagonist and the mentor engage in a training session, demonstrating their rapport and the mentor's ongoing guidance in the protagonist's magical or combat abilities.

<u>Strategic Discussion</u>
The protagonist and the mentor have a conversation about a mission, quest, or upcoming event, highlighting their trust in each other and the mentor's role in advising the protagonist.

<u>Shared Ritual</u>
The protagonist and the mentor participate in a magical ritual or ceremony together, showcasing their connection and shared beliefs or practices.

<u>Resuming Lessons</u>
The protagonist returns to the mentor after a period of absence, and their first scene together involves resuming their lessons or discussing new challenges the protagonist has encountered.

Family Gathering

The protagonist and the mentor attend a family gathering or celebration, emphasizing their shared history and the mentor's role as a family friend or relative.

Seeking Advice

The protagonist seeks out the mentor for advice on a personal matter, such as their developing romance or a dilemma they face, showcasing the trust and emotional bond between them.

Collaborating on a Project

The protagonist and the mentor work together on a project, such as researching a magical artifact or creating a new spell, highlighting their intellectual compatibility and teamwork.

Comforting Each Other

The protagonist and the mentor share a moment of vulnerability or loss, comforting each other and reinforcing their emotional bond.

Mentor's Test

The mentor challenges the protagonist with a test or task designed to measure their progress or push them to grow, illustrating the mentor's commitment to the protagonist's development.

Adventure Begins

The protagonist and the mentor set out together on a new adventure or quest, emphasizing their shared goals and the mentor's role in supporting the protagonist's journey.

How Can the Characters Spend Time Together?

Training and Lessons

The protagonist and the mentor engage in regular training sessions or lessons, whether in magical arts, combat skills, or diplomacy, fostering a deeper understanding of each other's strengths and weaknesses.

Sharing Stories

The protagonist and the mentor take turns sharing personal stories or recounting past experiences, including their families, adventures, and challenges they've faced, allowing them to understand each other on a deeper level and develop trust.

Research and Study
The protagonist and the mentor collaborate on research projects or study ancient texts, magical artifacts, or prophecies, showcasing their teamwork and intellectual compatibility.

Meditation and Reflection
The protagonist and the mentor practice meditation or other reflective exercises together, helping them to connect on a spiritual level and foster a deeper understanding of each other's beliefs and values.

Exploring the World
The protagonist and the mentor venture out into the world together, visiting enchanted places, magical cities, or sacred sites, allowing them to bond over shared experiences and learn from each other.

Resolving Conflicts
The protagonist and the mentor navigate conflicts or disputes, whether within their community or involving external parties, working together to find solutions and develop their problem-solving skills.

Magical Projects
The protagonist and the mentor collaborate on magical projects, such as creating new spells, potions, or enchantments, allowing them to learn from each other and grow their magical abilities.

Sharing Hobbies
The protagonist and the mentor share hobbies or interests, such as tending to magical creatures, gardening with magical plants, or crafting enchanted items, providing an opportunity for them to bond over shared passions.

Attending Events
The protagonist and the mentor attend magical events, festivals, or ceremonies together, offering a chance for them to learn more about each other's customs and traditions.

Guiding Through Challenges

The mentor supports the protagonist through personal challenges or emotional struggles, offering advice and guidance to help them navigate difficult situations and grow as a person.

The Protagonist
&
The Antagonist

What are ways the protagonist can meet the villain without them finding out that they are the villain?

Hidden Identity

The villain is disguised or concealing their identity when they first meet the protagonist, using a different name or appearance to avoid suspicion while interacting with the protagonist.

Friendly Encounter

The protagonist meets the villain in a seemingly innocent context, such as a social event, festival, or magical gathering, without being aware of the villain's ulterior motives or nefarious activities.

Common Goal

The protagonist and the villain temporarily share a common goal or enemy, leading them to work together or form a temporary alliance before the protagonist discovers the villain's true nature.

Misdirection

The villain pretends to be an ally or mentor, manipulating the protagonist into believing they have their best interests at heart while secretly furthering their own agenda.

Undercover Investigation

The protagonist encounters the villain while conducting an undercover investigation or spying mission, forcing them to maintain their cover while trying to gather information about the villain's true intentions.

Rescue Scenario

The villain saves the protagonist from a dangerous situation or magical creature, presenting themselves as a hero or protector and winning the protagonist's trust.

Shared Past

The protagonist and the villain have a shared past or connection, such as being childhood friends or former lovers, causing the protagonist to doubt or overlook the villain's dark side.

Unwitting Rivalry
The protagonist and the villain engage in a seemingly harmless
rivalry, such as a competition or magical duel, without the
protagonist realizing the villain's true intentions or the stakes
involved.

False Accusation
The villain is falsely accused of a crime or misdeed, causing the
protagonist to initially sympathize with or defend them, only to
later discover their true nature.

Benefactor Role
The villain poses as a benefactor, providing the protagonist with
resources, information, or magical assistance, while secretly using
them to advance their own goals.

How Can the Villain Trap the Protagonist?

Magical Imprisonment
The villain uses a powerful spell or enchantment to imprison the
protagonist in a magical cage, enchanted forest, or another realm,
preventing them from escaping or using their powers.

Hostage Situation
The villain kidnaps the protagonist's love interest or a close ally,
using them as leverage to force the protagonist into submission or
compliance with their demands.

Cursed Object
The protagonist becomes trapped or incapacitated by a cursed
object or artifact given to them by the villain, unknowingly binding
them to the villain's will or rendering them powerless.

Labyrinth or Maze
The villain lures the protagonist into a labyrinth or maze filled with
traps, magical barriers, or dangerous creatures, forcing the
protagonist to navigate a treacherous path to escape.

Forced Alliance

The villain blackmails or manipulates the protagonist into joining forces with them, threatening to expose a secret, harm a loved one, or bring about a catastrophe if the protagonist doesn't comply.

Time Loop or Stasis

The villain traps the protagonist in a time loop or magical stasis, forcing them to relive the same moments or events repeatedly, unable to change the outcome or break free from the cycle.

Magical Contract

The protagonist unwittingly enters into a magical contract or agreement with the villain, binding them to the villain's service or preventing them from taking action against the villain.

Dreamworld or Illusion

The villain traps the protagonist in a dreamworld or illusion, causing them to lose touch with reality and become lost in a fantastical world of the villain's creation.

Shapeshifting Deception

The villain uses shapeshifting or illusion magic to impersonate a trusted ally or the protagonist's love interest, deceiving the protagonist and leading them into a trap.

Hidden Fortress

The villain lures the protagonist to a hidden fortress or lair filled with magical defenses, traps, and minions, making it nearly impossible for the protagonist to escape or confront the villain.

The Protagonist
&
The Side Characters

The Protagonist and the Side Characters Meeting

<u>Unexpected Rescue</u>
The protagonist finds themselves in danger, perhaps from a magical beast or hostile entity, and the side character swoops in to save them.

<u>Chance Encounter</u>
The protagonist stumbles upon the side character in an unlikely place - perhaps a hidden corner of a magical library, an enchanted forest, or a secret market selling magical wares. The meeting seems coincidental but could be revealed later to be influenced by fate or a prophecy.

<u>Arranged Meeting</u>
The protagonist is summoned or sent by someone else (like a monarch, an elder, or a magical entity) to meet the side character. The side character might be a specialist in something the protagonist needs to learn about, a guide for their journey, or a key to unlocking their own hidden potential.

<u>Shared Goal/Purpose</u>
The protagonist and the side character cross paths because they are both seeking the same thing – perhaps a magical artifact, knowledge, or a person. They may decide to join forces, creating a dynamic of cooperation or competition.

<u>Inherited Servant or Companion</u>
The protagonist inherits a house, title, or artifact, and the side character comes with it. This side character might be a magical creature, a loyal servant, or a protective guardian who has been waiting for the protagonist.

<u>Rivals Turned Allies</u>
The protagonist and the side character start off as rivals, perhaps competing for a magical title or in a tournament. Over time, they find a mutual respect for each other and become allies, creating a complex relationship built on their past rivalry.

<u>Dreams or Visions</u>
The protagonist meets the side character in a dream or vision before meeting them in person. The side character might be a magical being who can communicate in dreams, or their meeting might be a prophetic vision of what's to come.

What if the Characters Already Know Each Other?

<u>Rekindling Old Ties</u>
The protagonist and side character could have been friends or lovers in the past but drifted apart due to a disagreement or circumstance. The story might then revolve around them rekindling their old relationship, overcoming past issues, and learning to trust each other again.

<u>Shared Secrets</u>
Both characters might share a secret or a hidden past that binds them together. This could be something like a forbidden magical practice, a shared crime, or knowledge about a significant event. Their efforts to protect this secret could lead to several intriguing plot developments.

<u>Changing Dynamics</u>
The protagonist and the side character might have known each other in a specific context (for instance, as teacher-student or master-servant). As the story progresses, this dynamic could shift dramatically - the student could surpass the teacher, or the servant could gain a position of power.

<u>Unrevealed Feelings</u>
One character could harbor secret feelings for the other. This could create tension and dramatic moments, especially if the feelings are revealed or reciprocated over the course of the story.

<u>Shared Trauma</u>
The characters could have experienced a traumatic event together in their past, influencing their relationship and their individual character arcs.

Rivalry
The characters might know each other as rivals. This rivalry could shift over the course of the story to friendship, mutual respect, or even romance.

Family Ties
The characters could be related, adding familial dynamics to their relationship. They might be siblings, cousins, or parent-child, with all the complexities that family relationships bring.

How Can the Characters Spend Time Together?

Training Sessions
If the side character is more experienced in certain aspects of the magical world, they might train the protagonist. These sessions could involve magic, combat, strategy, or even cultural norms of the magical world.

Joint Missions or Quests
The protagonist and the side character could be sent on missions or quests together.

Casual Socializing
Even in a fantasy world, characters will have downtime. They might eat meals together, enjoy a local festival, or engage in recreational activities like games or sports.

Research and Study
If there's a mystery to solve or a strategy to devise, the protagonist and side character might spend time researching together. This could be in a magical library, talking to wise beings, or exploring ancient ruins.

Travel
Journeying from one place to another can take considerable time in many fantasy worlds. Whether it's by foot, magical conveyance, or fantastical beast, the travel time gives characters plenty of opportunities to talk, bond, and face challenges together.

Caretaking
If one character falls ill or gets injured, the other might take care of them. This scenario can create intimate, vulnerable moments that deepen their relationship.

Shared Duty
The characters may share a duty or responsibility. This could be anything from protecting a magical artifact, taking care of magical creatures, or guarding a sacred place.

What are reasons the Side Character would need to explain the rules of the world?

Newcomer in a Strange Land
The protagonist, after being transported from the mundane world, lands in a parallel magical world. Here, a side character – perhaps a mystical creature or a local inhabitant – might need to explain the workings of magic, the rules governing its use, and the different fantastical races and creatures that inhabit the world.

Amnesia Scenario
The protagonist suffers from amnesia and can't remember the world they live in. A side character, possibly a close friend or a family member, needs to help them recall the magic system, the major historical events, and any magical abilities the protagonist may have forgotten.

Hidden Heritage
The protagonist is revealed to be part of a magical bloodline or species, unbeknownst to them. A side character, potentially a mentor or guide, explains their heritage and the implications it has on their place in the world, including any inherited powers, responsibilities, and the new social norms they must adhere to.

Rebellion Initiate
The protagonist joins a rebellion or secret society. The leader or another key member of the group must explain the political structure of the world, the power dynamics between different factions, and the true nature of the oppressive regime they're fighting against.

Magical Awakening
The protagonist's magical abilities manifest unexpectedly. A more experienced magic user takes them under their wing, explaining not just how magic works but also the different magical traditions, disciplines, and the potential dangers and ethical considerations they need to be aware of.

Forbidden Love
The protagonist falls in love with a creature from a different race or realm. Their lover, or a knowledgeable friend, explains the cultural practices, taboos, and potential consequences of their interspecies or interrealm romance, broadening the protagonist's understanding of the diverse societies within their world.

The Protagonist
&
World-Specific
Characters

The Protagonist and Meeting World Specific Characters

Summons or Invocation

The protagonist might use a magical ritual, spell, or artifact to summon or invoke a world-specific entity, like a spirit, deity, or magical creature. This could be intentional or accidental, depending on the protagonist's familiarity with the world's magic system.

Sacred Places

The protagonist might meet world-specific characters when they visit sacred or magical places, such as ancient temples, magical forests, or hidden realms. This could be a planned pilgrimage or an accidental stumble into a hidden world.

Visions or Dreams

Protagonists can encounter world-specific characters in their dreams or visions, especially if they possess certain magical abilities or if the entity wants to communicate a prophecy, warning, or piece of wisdom.

Magical Artifacts

Interacting with magical artifacts might transport the protagonist to another plane of existence, awaken a bound entity, or reveal a hidden character. These artifacts could be anything from a magical sword, a cursed book, to an enchanted mirror.

Historical Events

During a reenactment of historical events, a festival, or a ritual ceremony, world-specific characters such as ancient heroes, ancestral spirits, or deities might appear.

Guide

The protagonist might meet a world-specific character who becomes their guide to the magical world. This character might appear when the protagonist is in dire need, has reached a particular milestone, or has fulfilled certain conditions.

<u>Rescue</u>
The protagonist might save a world-specific character unknowingly, such as a magical creature in disguise, or release a character trapped in a spell, curse, or imprisonment.

What if the Characters Already Know Each Other?

<u>Ancient Pact or Bond</u>
The protagonist and the world-specific character might be bound by an ancient pact or bond, possibly made by their ancestors or even by the protagonist themselves in a forgotten past life.

<u>Family or Clan Ties</u>
The world-specific character might be a family member or part of the protagonist's clan. This could provide a deeply personal insight into the world's culture, traditions, and magical practices. The character might be a guardian spirit, an ancestral ghost, a shape-shifted relative, or a magical creature bound to serve the family.

<u>Shared Childhood or Past</u>
The protagonist and the world-specific character could have shared experiences from their past, such as growing up together or encountering each other during a significant event. The character might have been the protagonist's imaginary friend, a magical pet, or a mentor who guided them through early magical experiences.

<u>Sealed Memories</u>
The protagonist might have known the world-specific character in the past, but their memories of each other were sealed or erased due to a magical event, curse, or protective measure.

<u>Rites of Passage</u>
The protagonist, as part of their coming of age or induction into a magical order, might regularly commune with world-specific entities. This could involve periodic rituals, ceremonies, or meditations where they interact with these characters.

<u>Custodian of a Magical Entity</u>
The protagonist could be the guardian or caretaker of a world-specific character. This could be a magical creature, a trapped spirit, or even a sentient location.

How Can the Characters Spend Time Together?

Magical Training
If the world-specific character is more knowledgeable about the magic system or special abilities, they could spend time together training the protagonist.

Joint Missions
If the world-specific character has physical abilities or access to areas that the protagonist doesn't, they could embark on missions or quests together.

Rituals and Ceremonies
If the world-specific character is a spiritual or religious entity, they could spend time together in rituals, ceremonies, or worship practices. This might include anything from moon dances to sacrifice offerings, depending on your world's traditions.

Consultations and Conversations
The protagonist might spend time discussing their plans, problems, or thoughts with the world-specific character. These could be formal consultations, informal chats, or even internal dialogues if the character is a mental presence.

Guardianship or Stewardship
If the world-specific character is an entity, place, or item that the protagonist is responsible for, they could spend time together in caretaking activities. This might involve feeding a magical creature, maintaining a sacred place, or learning to use a magical item.

Rest and Recreation
Even in a fantastical setting, characters need time for leisure. They might spend time together stargazing, playing magical games, storytelling, or exploring the beauty of the magical world.

Dreams and Meditations
If the world-specific character is a spiritual or intangible entity, the protagonist could interact with them through dreams, visions, or meditations. This can provide a unique and mystical quality to their interactions.

Plotting Your Fantasy Romance

Structure
&
Development

Act 1

Setup

Introduction of the protagonist(s)

Introduce your main character(s) and establish their ordinary world. Highlight their desires, weaknesses, and strengths to make them relatable. The pacing should be steady, allowing the reader to connect with the protagonist(s).

> In the magical kingdom of Aellora, we meet Elara, a young and talented healer who lives with her family in a quaint village. We see her helping patients with her herbal remedies and empathetic nature, showcasing her compassionate and caring personality. In a nearby castle, we meet Prince Rowan, a restless and adventurous soul who feels confined by his royal duties and dreams of exploring the world. The ordinary world is established through their daily routines, struggles, and aspirations.

> In the bustling city of Ironport, we find Eamon, a blacksmith's apprentice who secretly practices elemental magic after hours. He has a kind heart and a penchant for helping others but struggles with his secret life. Meanwhile, we meet Lila, a scribe working in the city's archives, who is passionate about ancient magic and history. Their paths cross when Lila seeks Eamon's help in translating an ancient text, setting the stage for their initial meeting and a magical romance.

> In the enchanted forest of Eldor, we are introduced to Niamh, a half-elf archer and protector of her village. She is fierce, independent, and distrustful of outsiders. In a distant city, we meet Caelum, a mage who has grown tired of city life and yearns for a simpler existence. When an ancient artifact leads Caelum to Niamh's village, their worlds collide, and the ordinary world is established through their initial interactions and struggles to understand each other's cultures.

<u>Character Development</u>
Begin to flesh out your protagonist(s), love interest(s), and secondary characters. Show their personalities, relationships, and motivations, ensuring they feel well-rounded and engaging.

Backstory:
Develop the characters' backgrounds, including their family, upbringing, and significant life events that have shaped their personalities and motivations. This will help you create well-rounded, believable characters with depth.

> Elara grew up in a loving family of healers, learning the art of herbal remedies from her mother.

Physical Appearance:
Describe the characters' physical attributes, such as their age, height, build, hair and eye color, and any distinguishing features. This will help readers visualize your characters and make them more memorable.

> Elara has long, wavy red hair, bright green eyes, and a smattering of freckles across her cheeks.

Personality:
Determine your characters' key personality traits, strengths, and weaknesses. Consider their values, beliefs, and quirks. This will make them feel more real and relatable to your readers.

> Elara is compassionate, empathetic, and a bit shy, with a strong desire to help others.

Relationships:
Establish connections between your characters, such as friendships, rivalries, or family ties. This will provide a basis for character interactions and create opportunities for conflict and growth.

> Elara has a close relationship with her family and a best friend named Aria, who supports her in her healing work.

Goals and Motivations:
Identify what each character wants (their goals) and why they want
it (their motivations). This will help drive the story forward and
create natural opportunities for character development.

> Elara wants to become a renowned healer and find true
> love, driven by her passion for healing and her belief in the
> power of love.

Character Arcs:
Plan how your characters will change and grow throughout the
story. This may involve overcoming personal obstacles, learning
important lessons, or reevaluating their priorities. This will give your
story a strong emotional core and make it more satisfying for
readers.

> Throughout the story, Elara will learn to trust herself,
> overcome her shyness, and embrace her unique abilities.

Voice and Dialogue:
Give each character a unique voice that reflects their personality,
background, and emotions. This will help differentiate your
characters and make their dialogue feel authentic and engaging.

> Elara speaks softly and thoughtfully, often using herbal
> metaphors and expressing concern for others.

Roles in the Story:
Determine the roles your characters play in the story, whether they
are protagonists, love interests, allies, or antagonists. This will help
you understand their purpose in the narrative and how they
contribute to the story's progression.

> Elara is the protagonist and one of the love interests in the
> story.

<u>Inciting Incident</u>
Introduce an event that disrupts the protagonist's ordinary world
and sets the story in motion. In a romance fantasy, this could be a
magical encounter or the discovery of a hidden power. Maintain a
moderate pace to keep the reader engaged.

Elara and Prince Rowan
The inciting incident could be a mysterious illness that
sweeps through Elara's village, one that traditional
remedies can't cure. Prince Rowan hears about the
situation and arrives in the village, seeking Elara's help to
investigate the cause of the illness. Their partnership
brings them closer, setting the stage for a blossoming
romance amidst the challenges they face together.

Eamon and Lila
A powerful and dangerous artifact is discovered in the
city's archives, and Lila is tasked with finding a way to
safely contain or neutralize its magic. Knowing Eamon's
expertise in elemental magic, Lila enlists his help, forcing
him to reveal his secret life as a mage. As they work
together to unravel the artifact's mysteries, they find
themselves drawn to each other, igniting a romantic spark.

Niamh and Caelum
When an ancient evil threatens the enchanted forest of
Eldor, Niamh and her village must find a way to defend
themselves. Caelum, drawn to the village by the artifact he
possesses, inadvertently becomes entangled in their
struggle. Niamh and Caelum must set aside their
differences and work together to save the village, forging
an unexpected bond that develops into a deep and
passionate romance.

Meet-Cute
Introduce the love interest(s) in a memorable way, ideally around
the 10%-15% mark of the novel. This is where the romantic tension
between the characters begins to build. Develop the characters by
showcasing their personalities and unique traits.

Elara and Prince Rowan
Elara is out in the forest, gathering herbs for her remedies,
when she stumbles upon an injured animal. Unbeknownst
to her, the animal is actually Prince Rowan, who has been
temporarily transformed by a mischievous magical
creature. Elara tends to the animal's wounds, and when

Rowan returns to his human form, he is both grateful and captivated by her kindness and beauty.

Eamon and Lila
Lila is in the archives, searching for information on ancient magic, when she accidentally activates a magical trap hidden within one of the books. The trap releases a swarm of enchanted paper birds that wreak havoc in the archives. Eamon, who happens to be nearby, notices the chaos and rushes in to help. Using his elemental magic, he calms the paper birds, impressing Lila with his skills and sparking their initial connection.

Niamh and Caelum
Caelum, carrying the ancient artifact, unwittingly crosses into the enchanted forest of Eldor. Niamh, ever vigilant in her role as a protector, confronts him, believing him to be an intruder. They engage in a brief, spirited skirmish before realizing they are not enemies. Impressed by each other's skill and determination, they begin to form a mutual respect that serves as the foundation for their growing romance.

<u>World-Building</u>
Establish the rules and limitations of your fantasy world. Introduce magical elements, fantastical creatures, and the setting. Ensure the pacing allows for a thorough understanding of the world without overwhelming the reader.

Define the Magic System:
Establish the source of magic in your world, whether it's elemental, divine, or based on specific objects or rituals. Outline the rules governing how magic is learned, practiced, and controlled. Consider any limitations or consequences associated with using magic.

In Eamon and Lila's world, elemental magic is channeled through the user's connection to the natural elements (fire, water, earth, and air). Mages must undergo rigorous training to control their powers, and overuse of magic can lead to exhaustion or loss of control.

Introduce Fantastical Creatures:
Populate your world with unique and interesting creatures that fit the setting and tone of your story. Describe their appearances, habitats, behaviors, and any special abilities or characteristics they possess. Make sure these creatures impact the story, either directly or indirectly.

> In Niamh and Caelum's enchanted forest, various magical creatures coexist, such as talking animals, shape-shifting spirits, and mythical beasts. These creatures play an essential role in the characters' journey and the challenges they face.

Establish the Setting:
Describe the physical landscape, architecture, and climate of your fantasy world. Include details about its history, culture, and social structure. Create a sense of place that is vivid, immersive, and consistent throughout the story.

> In Elara and Prince Rowan's kingdom, there are lush forests, towering mountains, and quaint villages. The kingdom has a long history of magic and healing, which is deeply ingrained in its culture and traditions.

Introduce the Magical Elements Gradually:
Reveal the magical elements and rules of your world to the reader through the characters' experiences and interactions. Avoid overwhelming the reader with too much information at once. Instead, let the magical elements unfold naturally as the story progresses.

> As Elara and Prince Rowan work together to cure the mysterious illness, they encounter various magical challenges and learn more about the intricacies of their world's magical system.

Maintain Internal Consistency
Ensure that the rules and limitations of your fantasy world remain consistent throughout the story. This will help maintain the reader's suspension of disbelief and make your world feel more believable and immersive.

If it's established that a mage's power is limited by their energy reserves, make sure this rule applies to all mages throughout the story, including both protagonists and antagonists.

Call to Adventure

Around the 20%-25% mark of the novel, present a challenge or opportunity that pushes the protagonist(s) out of their comfort zone and into the fantasy world. This could be a quest, a prophecy, or a personal goal related to their newfound powers.

Elara and Prince Rowan

The call to adventure occurs when Elara and Prince Rowan discover that the mysterious illness plaguing the village is actually the result of a long-forgotten curse. They must embark on a perilous quest to find the cure, which lies hidden in a distant, magical land. As they face various challenges together, their bond strengthens, and their romance blossoms.

Eamon and Lila

As Eamon and Lila study the dangerous artifact, they uncover a hidden prophecy that foretells an imminent threat to their city. Together, they must embark on a journey to uncover ancient magical secrets that can help them neutralize the artifact's power and avert disaster. Along the way, their shared passion for magic and adventure brings them closer, igniting their romantic connection.

Niamh and Caelum

The call to adventure arrives when Niamh and Caelum learn that the ancient evil threatening the enchanted forest is actually a malevolent sorcerer seeking the power hidden within Caelum's artifact. They must join forces and embark on a dangerous quest to stop the sorcerer and protect their world. As they face adversity together, their initial mistrust transforms into a deep, passionate love.

Character Goals and Motivations

Clearly establish the goals and motivations of your protagonist(s) and love interest(s). These goals should be both personal (e.g., self-

140

discovery or personal growth) and external (e.g., saving the world or solving a mystery).

Elara and Prince Rowan

Before embarking on their quest, Elara and Prince Rowan have a heartfelt conversation about their fears and hopes. Elara expresses her determination to save her village and uphold her family's legacy as healers, while Prince Rowan reveals his desire to prove his worth as a leader and protector. This shared commitment to their goals helps establish a strong bond between the characters and sets the stage for their romantic journey.

Eamon and Lila

As Eamon and Lila prepare for their mission, they discuss the personal stakes involved. Eamon is driven by his desire to protect the city and finally embrace his identity as a mage, while Lila seeks to preserve the knowledge and history contained within the archives. Their shared passion for magic and their determination to prevent disaster create a strong connection that lays the groundwork for their developing romance.

Niamh and Caelum

Before setting out on their quest, Niamh and Caelum have a moment of reflection. Niamh, driven by her duty to protect her village and preserve the enchanted forest, is determined to face the sorcerer and restore peace. Caelum, motivated by a desire to atone for his past mistakes and unlock the true power of the artifact, is committed to supporting Niamh and their shared cause. As their motivations align, their initial mistrust begins to evolve into a deeper emotional connection.

Foreshadowing and Subplots

Plant seeds for future conflicts or revelations. Introduce subplots that will become important later in the story. Ensure the pacing remains steady, allowing the reader to absorb these details without feeling overwhelmed.

Elara and Prince Rowan

Before embarking on their quest, Elara and Prince Rowan hear rumors about a dangerous creature guarding the cure they seek. Although they don't know the full extent of the danger, this information plants the seed for a future conflict. Additionally, Prince Rowan seems hesitant to share something about his past. This unresolved tension hints at a future revelation that could affect their relationship.

Eamon and Lila

As Eamon and Lila research the artifact, they come across an obscure reference to an ancient magical order that may have hidden knowledge about the artifact. This information plants the seed for a future revelation and potential conflict as they uncover more about this secretive group. Furthermore, Lila seems to be keeping a secret about her family's history, which may cause tension between her and Eamon when the truth is revealed.

Niamh and Caelum

Before setting out on their journey, Niamh and Caelum learn about an enigmatic prophecy tied to the artifact, but they don't yet understand its full implications. This hint foreshadows a significant revelation that could impact their quest and relationship. Additionally, there's an underlying tension between Niamh's village and Caelum's people, suggesting a possible conflict that could arise as they work together.

Initial Obstacles

As the protagonist(s) begin to grapple with the challenges presented by the inciting incident and the call to adventure, introduce initial obstacles or conflicts. These can be small-scale and personal or larger, external conflicts that foreshadow the main antagonistic force.

Elara and Prince Rowan

As Elara and Prince Rowan prepare for their journey, they face opposition from the village elders, who worry about the consequences of sending their beloved healer away.

Additionally, Elara must come to terms with leaving her home for the first time, while Prince Rowan grapples with the responsibilities of leadership. These initial conflicts allow the characters to prove their commitment to their quest and develop a deeper bond as they support each other through these challenges.

Eamon and Lila
Eamon and Lila encounter difficulties in accessing the secretive knowledge they need to neutralize the artifact, forcing them to navigate the city's hidden magical underground. As they work together to overcome these obstacles, their initial impressions of each other are challenged, allowing them to see new aspects of each other's personalities. These conflicts help build trust and rapport between the characters, laying the foundation for their romantic relationship.

Niamh and Caelum
Before they can embark on their quest, Niamh and Caelum must convince their respective communities to put aside their longstanding animosity and work together to face the sorcerer's threat. This conflict tests their diplomatic and leadership skills, while also providing opportunities for them to learn more about each other's backgrounds and motivations. As they overcome these initial obstacles, their respect for each other grows, creating a strong emotional connection that deepens into love.

<u>Crossing the Threshold</u>
The protagonist(s) commit to their journey and enter the fantastical world. They may face initial opposition or obstacles. Keep the pacing brisk to maintain tension and excitement.

Elara and Prince Rowan
Elara and Prince Rowan cross the threshold when they leave the village together, entering a vast and uncharted wilderness in search of the cure. As they venture deeper into the unknown, they encounter dangerous creatures and enchanted landscapes, testing their courage and resourcefulness. Their shared experiences and reliance on

each other in the face of adversity strengthen their bond, allowing their romantic relationship to evolve.

Eamon and Lila
Eamon and Lila cross the threshold when they discover a hidden entrance to an ancient, magical library containing the knowledge they seek. As they delve deeper into the library, they must navigate a series of magical traps and puzzles, testing their wit and magical abilities. Working as a team and facing these challenges together not only advances their quest but also deepens their emotional connection, fueling their budding romance.

Niamh and Caelum
Niamh and Caelum cross the threshold when they secure the reluctant cooperation of their respective communities and set off on their quest to confront the malevolent sorcerer. As they journey through the enchanted forest and beyond, they face various trials, such as navigating treacherous terrain, battling powerful magical foes, and overcoming personal fears. As they rely on each other's strengths and support each other through their weaknesses, their bond grows stronger, and their love deepens.

Close Act 1 with a decision or event that propels the protagonist(s) into Act 2. This should involve the protagonist(s) making a commitment to their journey or facing a point of no return. The pacing should pick up here to create a sense of urgency and excitement.

<u>Act 2</u>

Confrontation

<u>Trials and Tribulations</u>

Throughout the first half of Act 2, the protagonist(s) and love interest(s) face a series of tests, both physical and emotional. These trials should develop the characters, deepen their relationship, and strengthen their bond. Vary the pacing to create a balance between action and introspection.

Elara and Prince Rowan

As Elara and Prince Rowan journey through the wilderness, they face various challenges, such as surviving harsh weather conditions, finding food and shelter, and battling fearsome creatures. These trials test their courage, trust, and teamwork, revealing hidden strengths and vulnerabilities. When Elara saves Rowan from a dangerous creature, and Rowan helps Elara overcome her fear of heights, they realize they can rely on each other, deepening their bond and love for one another.

Eamon and Lila

While exploring the ancient library, Eamon and Lila encounter magical traps, riddles, and illusions that test their intellect, magical abilities, and trust in each other. As they work together to overcome these obstacles, they learn to appreciate each other's unique skills and insights. When Lila reveals her family secret, and Eamon shares his past struggles, they become more vulnerable with each other, allowing their relationship to grow stronger and more intimate.

Niamh and Caelum

As Niamh and Caelum traverse the enchanted forest and beyond, they face various trials, such as navigating treacherous terrain, solving mystical riddles, and confronting powerful magical creatures. These challenges test their resilience, resourcefulness, and compatibility, forcing them to rely on each other's strengths and support.

When Niamh helps Caelum confront his past, and Caelum
supports Niamh in a moment of self-doubt, they realize
their bond is more than just a partnership, and their love
for each other deepens.

<u>Deepening the Romance</u>
As the characters navigate the trials, their romantic feelings and
attraction grow. This is where the "will they or won't they?" tension
comes into play. Use pacing to build anticipation and intensify the
romantic tension, with the midpoint as the climax of this
development.

Elara and Prince Rowan
Throughout their journey, Elara and Prince Rowan share
intimate conversations, stolen glances, and tender
moments that heighten their romantic tension. As they
learn to trust each other and face challenges together,
their attraction becomes undeniable. At the midpoint of
the story, they find themselves trapped in a cave during a
storm, and the emotional intensity of their situation leads
to a passionate, unexpected kiss. This moment marks a
turning point in their relationship, signaling that their
feelings have evolved beyond mere companionship.

Eamon and Lila
As Eamon and Lila solve riddles and navigate magical traps,
they grow closer, sharing laughter, playful banter, and
meaningful conversations. Their intellectual connection
deepens, and they find themselves increasingly drawn to
each other. At the midpoint, they accidentally trigger a
magical enchantment that forces them to confront their
feelings, resulting in a powerful, emotionally charged
embrace. This moment solidifies their romantic bond and
signals a shift in their relationship.

Niamh and Caelum
Throughout their quest, Niamh and Caelum's trust and
respect for each other develop into a deeper emotional
connection. They share vulnerable moments, such as
Niamh confiding in Caelum about her fears for the
enchanted forest and Caelum opening up about the guilt

he carries from his past. At the midpoint, they find a hidden sanctuary where they let their guard down, and under the glow of a magical moon, they share their first tender kiss. This moment marks a significant turning point in their relationship, as they acknowledge and embrace their growing love.

<u>Midpoint</u>
Around the 50% mark of the novel, reach a turning point in the story where the protagonist(s) and love interest(s) confront their feelings for one another. This could be a moment of intimacy, a confession of love, or a significant change in their relationship. Slow down the pacing to allow the emotional impact to resonate.

Elara and Prince Rowan
After the passionate kiss in the cave, Elara and Prince Rowan find themselves in a quiet forest glade, where they take a moment to rest and reflect on their journey so far. The slower pace allows them to openly discuss their feelings for each other and the potential consequences of pursuing a relationship. Their conversation is filled with tender moments, lingering glances, and gentle touches, allowing the emotional impact of their love to resonate with the reader.

Eamon and Lila
Following their emotionally charged embrace, Eamon and Lila find a secluded corner of the library where they can escape the magical traps and riddles. The slower pace of this scene allows them to delve deeper into their feelings, exploring their fears, hopes, and dreams together. As they share intimate stories and vulnerabilities, their connection grows stronger, and the emotional impact of their budding romance is amplified for the reader.

Niamh and Caelum
After their tender kiss under the magical moon, Niamh and Caelum decide to spend the night at the hidden sanctuary, away from the dangers of their quest. The slower pace of this moment allows them to fully express their feelings for one another and contemplate the future of their

relationship. As they hold each other close and share whispered words of love, the emotional intensity of their bond is heightened, allowing the reader to experience the depth of their connection.

<u>Antagonist(s) and Conflict</u>
In the second half of Act 2, introduce or develop the antagonist(s) who challenge the protagonist(s) and/or the romantic relationship. The conflict can stem from internal or external sources, such as a rival love interest or a villain threatening the fantasy world. Adjust the pacing to create a sense of urgency and heighten the stakes.

Elara and Prince Rowan
As Elara and Prince Rowan continue their journey, a rival kingdom learns of their quest for the cure and sends a cunning and ruthless agent to thwart their efforts. The agent's arrival accelerates the pacing and heightens the stakes, forcing Elara and Rowan to navigate a series of dangerous encounters and traps. Their love is put to the test as they face these new challenges and struggle to protect both their mission and each other.

Eamon and Lila
While Eamon and Lila grow closer, they discover the existence of a power-hungry sorcerer who seeks to harness the artifact's power for his own nefarious purposes. The sorcerer's pursuit of the artifact raises the stakes and injects a sense of urgency into the story, as Eamon and Lila must decipher the ancient knowledge and neutralize the artifact before it falls into the wrong hands. Their love and trust are put to the test as they race against time and confront the sorcerer's sinister machinations.

Niamh and Caelum
As Niamh and Caelum's love deepens, the malevolent sorcerer they seek to confront learns of their alliance and sends dark forces to sabotage their quest. The increased threat creates a sense of urgency and raises the stakes, as the couple must face powerful magical foes and protect their communities from the sorcerer's sinister influence. Their love is challenged as they fight together against these

forces, testing their bond and determination to save their
world.

<u>Subplots and Secondary Characters</u>
Continue to develop subplots and secondary characters that
support the main story arc. Their development should intersect
with the main plot and contribute to the overall tension and stakes.
Maintain a steady pace to keep the reader engaged without
overwhelming them.

Elara and Prince Rowan
As Elara and Rowan face the challenges presented by the
rival kingdom's agent, a subplot involving Rowan's younger
sister, Princess Isla, unfolds. Isla, who is eager to prove her
worth, embarks on a secret mission to aid her brother and
Elara, forming an alliance with a skilled tracker. The subplot
featuring Isla and the tracker not only provides additional
challenges and allies for the main characters but also
reveals important information about the rival kingdom's
plans, directly impacting the main plot and increasing the
stakes.

Eamon and Lila
As Eamon and Lila race against time to decipher the
ancient knowledge and neutralize the artifact, a subplot
involving Lila's estranged brother, who is secretly working
for the power-hungry sorcerer, comes into play. Lila's
brother's conflicting loyalties add tension and emotional
complexity to the main plot. As Lila tries to reconnect with
her brother, his ultimate decision to either help or betray
the protagonists directly influences the outcome of their
quest, contributing to the overall tension and stakes.

Niamh and Caelum
While Niamh and Caelum confront the dark forces sent by
the malevolent sorcerer, a subplot involving a group of
secondary characters from both communities emerges.
These characters form a secret alliance to support Niamh
and Caelum's quest, gathering vital information and
resources. Their actions, both courageous and at times
misguided, add an additional layer of intrigue and conflict

149

to the main plot. The subplot with these secondary characters not only highlights the unity between the two communities but also plays a crucial role in the story's climax.

<u>Character Development</u>
Use the challenges and conflicts in Act 2 to show how the protagonist(s) and love interest(s) grow and evolve as individuals and as a couple. Reveal their vulnerabilities, strengths, and transformations as they face adversity.

Elara and Prince Rowan
As Elara and Prince Rowan face the rival kingdom's agent and the various dangers on their journey, they learn to rely on each other's strengths and support each other's weaknesses. Elara discovers her latent magical abilities, while Rowan learns to embrace his strategic instincts and diplomacy. As they grow individually, their shared experiences and challenges also bring them closer together, solidifying their trust and love for one another in the face of adversity.

Eamon and Lila
Throughout their quest to decipher the ancient knowledge and neutralize the artifact, Eamon and Lila confront their own insecurities and fears. Eamon learns to trust in his own intelligence and innate magical talents, while Lila comes to terms with her family's secret and embraces her role as a protector of knowledge. As they grow as individuals, their relationship deepens, with each character's personal growth complementing the other's. Their evolving bond enables them to face the challenges posed by the power-hungry sorcerer with unity and strength.

Niamh and Caelum
As Niamh and Caelum confront the dark forces and magical threats sent by the malevolent sorcerer, they each face their own internal struggles. Niamh learns to trust her instincts and leadership abilities, while Caelum confronts his past and finds redemption in his actions. As they evolve

individually, their connection and love deepen, forging a strong partnership that allows them to face the sorcerer's challenges with courage and determination.

<u>All is Lost</u>
Around the 75% mark of the novel, reach a low point in the story where the protagonist(s) suffer a major setback or loss. This can be a breakup, a betrayal, or a failure in their quest. Slow the pacing to emphasize the emotional weight of the situation and allow the characters to reflect on their journey.

Elara and Prince Rowan
Elara and Prince Rowan, while attempting to retrieve the final ingredient for the cure, are betrayed by a seemingly trusted ally. As a result, they become separated, and Elara is captured by the rival kingdom's agent. The pacing slows down, allowing both characters to reflect on their journey and realize the depth of their love for each other. This moment of despair and separation fuels their determination to reunite and complete their quest, no matter the cost.

Eamon and Lila
Eamon and Lila, just as they believe they've successfully deciphered the ancient knowledge and are on the verge of neutralizing the artifact, find out that Lila's brother has stolen it and delivered it to the power-hungry sorcerer. This betrayal and loss force the characters to confront their deepest fears and insecurities. As the pacing slows, Eamon and Lila take time to reflect on their journey and the strength they draw from their love, which inspires them to pursue the artifact and face the sorcerer together.

Niamh and Caelum
As Niamh and Caelum prepare to confront the malevolent sorcerer, they suffer a devastating loss when their secret alliance is discovered, and several of their friends are captured or killed. This low point in the story serves to emphasize the emotional weight of their journey and the sacrifices made along the way. The pacing slows as Niamh and Caelum grieve for their fallen friends and draw

strength from their love for each other, vowing to defeat the sorcerer and restore peace to their communities.

<u>Dark Night of the Soul</u>
Following the "all is lost" moment, the protagonist(s) and love interest(s) face their darkest moments, questioning their beliefs, motivations, and the possibility of success. Use this introspective period to deepen the reader's emotional connection with the characters.

Elara and Prince Rowan
Separated and feeling defeated, Elara and Rowan begin to doubt their abilities and the viability of their quest. Elara, while captive, questions her newfound magical powers and wonders if she's strong enough to escape and reunite with Rowan. Meanwhile, Rowan wrestles with feelings of guilt over Elara's capture and doubts his worthiness as a leader. This introspective period allows readers to empathize with their emotional struggles, strengthening their connection to the characters. Ultimately, their love and determination inspire them to overcome their doubts, setting the stage for a thrilling third act.

Eamon and Lila
Reeling from the betrayal and loss of the artifact, Eamon and Lila question their motivations and the chances of retrieving the artifact from the power-hungry sorcerer. Eamon grapples with self-doubt, unsure if he can harness his magical talents effectively, while Lila wrestles with her family's past and the consequences of her brother's actions. As they work through their emotions, readers become more invested in their journey. The love and trust between Eamon and Lila ultimately bolster their resolve, leading them into the climactic third act.

Niamh and Caelum
In the wake of their friends' deaths and the discovery of their secret alliance, Niamh and Caelum question their own beliefs and the feasibility of defeating the malevolent sorcerer. Niamh wonders if she can truly unite the two communities, while Caelum doubts his ability to overcome

his dark past. This introspective period deepens the reader's emotional connection with the characters as they confront their darkest fears. Through their love and shared experiences, Niamh and Caelum find renewed strength and determination, propelling them into the final act.

Close Act 2 with a catalyst that propels the protagonist(s) towards the climax in Act 3. This can be a revelation, a decision, or a newfound determination to overcome the obstacles and achieve their goals. The pacing should pick up to create a sense of urgency and anticipation as the story moves into Act 3.

Act 3

Resolution

<u>Climax Preparations</u>

Begin Act 3 with the protagonist(s) regaining their resolve and preparing for the final confrontation. They might gather allies, resources, or learn critical information that will help them face the antagonist(s). Keep the pacing brisk to maintain tension and excitement.

Elara and Prince Rowan

Elara, tapping into her newfound magical abilities, manages to escape her captors and reunites with Rowan, who has rallied his remaining allies. Together, they gather vital resources and information about the rival kingdom's plans. The brisk pacing keeps readers engaged as Elara and Rowan make their final preparations to face the rival kingdom's agent and secure the last ingredient for the cure, culminating in an epic battle.

Eamon and Lila

With renewed determination, Eamon and Lila follow a crucial lead to the sorcerer's lair, enlisting the help of their remaining friends and allies. Along the way, they uncover hidden knowledge that could turn the tide in their favor. The brisk pacing maintains tension as they race against time to retrieve the stolen artifact and confront the power-hungry sorcerer, setting the stage for an intense magical showdown.

Niamh and Caelum

Niamh and Caelum, bolstered by their love and shared experiences, rally the surviving members of their secret alliance, and gather vital intelligence about the malevolent sorcerer's plans. As they prepare to face the dark forces, they also work to unite their communities, strengthening their bond and resolve. The pacing remains brisk, keeping readers excited and invested as Niamh and Caelum lead their allies into a climactic battle to restore peace and bring down the sorcerer.

Climax

Around the 85%-90% mark of the novel, the protagonist(s) confront the antagonist(s) or overcome the main conflict in an epic, final showdown. This could be a battle, a magical duel, or a daring rescue. Increase the pacing to create a sense of urgency and excitement during this climactic moment.

Elara and Prince Rowan

In a high-stakes confrontation, Elara and Prince Rowan face off against the rival kingdom's agent and their forces in a fierce battle. The pacing increases to emphasize the urgency and excitement of the showdown. With Elara's newfound magical powers and Rowan's strategic prowess, they outmaneuver the enemy and secure the final ingredient for the cure. Their love and trust in each other play a vital role in their success, solidifying their bond as they triumph over adversity.

Eamon and Lila

Eamon and Lila, along with their allies, infiltrate the sorcerer's lair in a daring rescue mission to retrieve the stolen artifact. The pacing picks up, creating a tense and thrilling atmosphere as they navigate the sorcerer's traps and confront his minions. In a climactic magical duel, Eamon and Lila use their combined knowledge and power to outwit the power-hungry sorcerer and neutralize the artifact, saving their world from destruction.

Niamh and Caelum

Niamh and Caelum lead their alliance in a massive battle against the malevolent sorcerer and his dark forces. The pacing accelerates, heightening the urgency and excitement of the confrontation. As they fight side by side, their love and unity inspire their forces, turning the tide in their favor. In a decisive moment, Niamh and Caelum use their combined strengths to defeat the sorcerer, restoring peace and unity to their communities.

<u>The Power of Love</u>
The protagonist(s) and love interest(s) reconcile and realize the importance of their love for one another. Love may serve as the key to overcoming the obstacles they face. Slow the pacing to allow for emotional depth and reflection as the characters express their feelings and find strength in their bond.

Elara and Prince Rowan
After their triumphant victory, Elara and Rowan share a tender moment, reflecting on the challenges they overcame and the love that grew between them. The pacing slows, allowing the reader to fully appreciate the emotional depth of their connection. They recognize how their love served as the key to their success, and they pledge their lives to each other, vowing to rule the kingdom together with wisdom and compassion.

Eamon and Lila
With the stolen artifact neutralized and the sorcerer defeated, Eamon and Lila take a moment to acknowledge the importance of their love. As the pacing slows, they express their feelings, realizing that their love and trust in one another were instrumental in overcoming the obstacles they faced. They decide to dedicate their lives to preserving ancient knowledge and supporting one another as partners in both love and magic.

Niamh and Caelum
Following the sorcerer's defeat and the restoration of peace, Niamh and Caelum share a heartfelt conversation, reflecting on their journey and the love that blossomed between them. The pacing slows, giving the characters and the reader a chance to savor the emotional depth of their relationship. They recognize that their love was the key to uniting their communities, and together, they commit to leading their people into a new era of harmony.

<u>Resolution</u>
With the conflict resolved, the characters' new status quo is established. Loose ends are tied up, and any lingering questions are addressed. Allow the pacing to slow down, giving the reader a

chance to process the story's events and witness the consequences of the climax.

Elara and Prince Rowan

As the kingdom celebrates the cure's discovery and the newfound alliance, Elara and Rowan settle into their roles as rulers. The pacing slows, allowing readers to witness the positive changes their love has brought to the kingdom. Secondary characters find their own resolutions, and lingering questions about the characters' futures are answered. The story concludes with a royal wedding, symbolizing the union of the two kingdoms and the promise of a brighter future.

Eamon and Lila

With the sorcerer defeated and the artifact safe, Eamon and Lila dedicate themselves to preserving magical knowledge and rebuilding their community. The pacing slows, offering readers a glimpse into their new life together. Subplots involving secondary characters reach their conclusions, and any remaining questions are resolved. The story ends with Eamon and Lila opening a school of magic, ensuring that their love and shared passion will continue to shape their world.

Niamh and Caelum

As peace returns to their communities, Niamh and Caelum work together to heal old wounds and promote unity. The pacing slows, showing readers the progress they've made and the impact of their love on the two communities. Secondary characters find their own resolutions, and lingering questions about the protagonists' roles in the new order are answered. The story concludes with a celebration of unity, marking the beginning of a new era of peace and cooperation.

Character Development and Growth

Show the growth and transformation of the protagonist(s) and love interest(s) throughout Act 3. They should emerge from the story as changed individuals, having learned from their experiences, and grown as a result of their journey.

Elara and Prince Rowan
Throughout Act 3, Elara and Rowan demonstrate their growth as individuals and as a couple. Elara has embraced her magical abilities and newfound confidence, while Rowan has learned to trust his instincts and the value of collaboration. United by love, they have become strong, compassionate leaders who are ready to rule their kingdom together. Their personal growth and the strength of their bond ultimately secure the future of their people and the success of their alliance.

Eamon and Lila
In Act 3, Eamon and Lila's journey showcases their growth as individuals and as a couple. Eamon has learned to accept his magical heritage and the responsibility that comes with it, while Lila has discovered her own strength and courage. Together, they have overcome their fears and insecurities, forging a partnership based on love, trust, and shared passion. Their transformation leads them to create a new life dedicated to preserving ancient knowledge and nurturing future generations of magic-users.

Niamh and Caelum
Throughout Act 3, Niamh and Caelum evolve as individuals and as a couple. Niamh has grown into a wise, empathetic leader, while Caelum has found the courage to defy tradition and embrace change. United by their love, they have become a symbol of hope and unity for their communities. Their growth and the strength of their bond enable them to overcome adversity and usher in a new era of peace, cooperation, and prosperity for their people.

Subplots and Secondary Characters
Resolve any remaining subplots and provide closure for secondary characters. Ensure that their storylines are wrapped up in a satisfying way that adds to the overall story.

Elara and Prince Rowan
In the aftermath of the final battle, the secondary characters also find resolution. Elara's mentor, who has guided her throughout her magical journey, receives

recognition for his wisdom and dedication. Rowan's loyal advisor, who has supported him in his quest for peace, is appointed to a key position in the new government. Elara's best friend, who has been her confidante during her struggles, finds her own calling as a talented healer. These resolutions underscore the importance of teamwork and loyalty, adding depth to the main story.

Eamon and Lila

As Eamon and Lila establish their new life together, their secondary characters also experience closure. Eamon's estranged family members reconcile with him, acknowledging his bravery and accepting his magical abilities. Lila's mentor, who has been a source of guidance and wisdom, retires with honor, confident that her teachings will live on through her protégé. The young apprentice who helped them on their journey discovers his own magical talents, foreshadowing a promising future. These subplots reinforce themes of forgiveness, understanding, and personal growth.

Niamh and Caelum

As peace is restored to their communities, secondary characters find their own resolutions. Niamh's wise elder, who has counseled her throughout her journey, sees the fruits of her guidance in the united communities. Caelum's rebellious sister, who has challenged tradition alongside him, takes on a leadership role, working to bridge the gap between the two communities. A supporting character who had been caught in the conflict between the groups finds love and acceptance in the new era of peace. These resolutions highlight the importance of change, understanding, and cooperation.

<u>Final Revelations or Twists</u>

If you have any final surprises or revelations in store, reveal them towards the end of Act 3, but before the final wrap-up. These should not overshadow the resolution, but rather enhance the story and provide a sense of completeness.

Elara and Prince Rowan
Just before the final wrap-up, it is revealed that the
magical cure discovered earlier not only heals the afflicted
but also boosts the magical abilities of those who possess
them. This revelation provides a sense of hope and wonder
for the kingdom's future, reinforcing the importance of
love, unity, and understanding between the two nations.

Eamon and Lila
As they establish their new school of magic, Eamon and
Lila uncover a hidden library filled with ancient magical
texts and artifacts. This surprise discovery provides a sense
of awe and excitement, highlighting the importance of
preserving knowledge and the limitless possibilities that lie
ahead for the protagonists and their students.

Niamh and Caelum
In the final stages of the story, it is revealed that the two
communities share a common ancestry, which was lost to
history due to a long-standing conflict. This revelation
strengthens the bond between the communities and adds
depth to the story, emphasizing the importance of unity,
understanding, and rediscovering lost connections.

<u>Happy, Ever After (or not)</u>
The protagonist(s) and love interest(s) reach the conclusion of their
romantic journey, which should occur around the 95%-100% mark
of the novel. This could be a happy ending, a tragic sacrifice, or
something bittersweet. It's up to you to decide the fate of their love
story. Allow the pacing to slow down, giving the reader time to
savor the emotional impact of the ending.

Elara and Prince Rowan
Elara and Rowan's love story concludes with a grand
wedding ceremony that unites their kingdoms and marks
the beginning of a new era of peace and prosperity. As the
protagonists stand before their people, they pledge their
love and commitment to each other, promising to lead
their kingdom with wisdom and compassion. The reader is
left with a sense of hope, joy, and the power of love to
heal and transform.

Eamon and Lila

Eamon and Lila's love story reaches a bittersweet ending as they decide to leave their old lives behind to create a new school of magic, dedicated to preserving ancient knowledge and nurturing future generations of magic-users. While they must part from their families and friends, their love and shared passion for their mission provide them with the strength and inspiration to embrace their new life together. The reader is left with a sense of sacrifice, new beginnings, and the power of love to inspire change.

Niamh and Caelum

Niamh and Caelum's love story concludes with a tragic sacrifice, as Caelum gives his life to protect Niamh and their people during the final confrontation with the antagonist. Niamh, heartbroken but resolute, honors his memory by dedicating her life to building a peaceful, unified world where their love story serves as a symbol of hope and unity. The reader is left with a sense of loss, resilience, and the power of love to endure and inspire.

Thank you for reading and I hope this helps that writer's block and you can continue writing a beautifully crafted love story.

New books are coming out every month, to stay informed, feel free to join my mailing list at www.thebetfordcollection.com.

Other Books in the Series

Fantasy Romance Writing: The Magical Guide to World-Building